PRAISE FOR
THE YOGA OF SELF-LOVE

The Yoga of Self-Love is a memoir steeped in wisdom, and ultimately a roadmap toward deepened self-knowing and a return to love. Its epiphanies come with rare clarity from a life that doesn't avert its gaze from the truths the author seeks––even when those truths are hard ones. Writing from the fine edge of vulnerability and with an openness that draws us all in, Ramaa draws from the deep well of her own memories and heartaches and finds ballast in a tapestry of insights from multiple learned and sacred traditions. Read in one swift gulp, or taken sip by sip, it's a book that will stay with you and just might bring you home along the way."

Barbara Mahany, essayist and author of *The Book of Nature: The Astonishing Beauty of God's First Sacred Text*

"Read *The Yoga of Self-Love* and benefit from the wisdom of age-old truths and modern personal growth tools. Ramaa Krishnan beautifully opens up and shares her inspiring story so that we readers may benefit from the deep personal healing work she has done. Questions for Reflection in each chapter will draw you in and help you apply Ramaa's powerful tools and insights to your own healing and cultivation of well-being. You'll learn to clear old beliefs so that you can embrace new, life-affirming ones, and to cultivate a new and loving relationship with your inner child, freeing you from the inevitable wounds of childhood."

Lisa Tener, author of *Breathe. Write. Breathe.: 18 Energizing Practices to Spark Your Writing and Free Your Voice*

"*The Yoga of Self-Love* is a mesmerizing and captivating journey exploring Ramaa Krishnan's journey to self-discovery. Ramaa is a masterful guide to self-awareness. Her combination of Eastern philosophy and Western psychology leads to a compelling, thought-provoking read. In a world that focuses on the outside in, Ramaa's journey is to heal her inner child as she explores guilt, shame, fear, and many more emotions along her journey from fear to faith. This book is a must read for anyone on the road to revelation and growth."

Wendy Dolin, founder of Medication-Induced Suicide Prevention and Education Foundation (MISSD), licensed clinical social worker, and certified family therapist

"Ramaa offers readers a blessed gift with her insightful and engaging book/workbook. A gifted writer and counselor with inspiring courage, Ramaa invites us on her personal pilgrimage as she uncovers the mysteries of self-awareness and joy-filled discovery. *The Yoga of Self-love* is a perfect companion for our journey in these challenging times."

      Andrea White, EdD, president of People Focus

"Thank you for writing this gorgeous book. This is a book of becoming, especially as a divine feminine being. Thank you for weaving and lighting the way. Readers will be educated, inspired, touched, and deeply cared for, should they wish to find their own ways. Brava—and more please!"

      Jennifer Stith, executive director of Wings, Supporting Adult Survivors of Childhood Sexual Abuse, trauma-informed, somatic-based coach, and consultant

"Ramaa shares her hero's journey in a way that is compelling, heartwarming, and entertaining. She deftly weaves in elements from Kundalini yoga, Carl Jung's work, sacred Hindu text, and English fables, distilling complex teachings into digestible nuggets of wisdom. She also courageously shares the depth of her own inner experience in a way that inspires the reader to apply her journey of spiritual growth to their own life. This is a must read for anyone interested in moving forward and taking responsibility for their own well-being."

      Maren Deaver, LCSW, NARM master therapist

"Ramaa is a deeply authentic individual and an artist with beautiful words and memories for which she shares with her heart and soul in this book. From her healing journey we learn how to build relationships with others and most importantly ourselves. I highly recommend this book to help us achieve growth in all areas of life."

      Deb Guy, director of Women's Exchange

"Providing tools after each chapter for our own self-love journey, Krishnan generously shares her own story. With humility and profound willingness to seek and grow, she models the way home to an authentic life. An effortless storyteller. A born teacher. A lifelong seeker."

      Amy Matheny, vice president of sales at *Chicago Reader*

THE YOGA of SELF-LOVE

THE YOGA *of* SELF-LOVE

The Sacred Path *to* Wholeness *and* Healing through Inner-Child Work

Ramaa Krishnan

The Yoga of Self-Love
The Sacred Path to Wholeness and Healing through Inner-Child Work

Ramaa Krishnan

ISBN: 979-8-9910080-0-6
Library of Congress Control Number: 2024914510

Published by Full Bloomed Lotus Center for Self-Awareness
www.fullbloomedlotus.com

Copyright © 2024 by Ramaa Krishnan. All rights reserved. Unless otherwise noted, no part of this book may be reproduced, stored in a retrieval system, transmitted in any form or by any means, electronic, mechanical photocopying, or recording without express written permission from the author, except for brief quotations or critical reviews. For more information, please contact Ramaa Krishnan at ramaa@ fullbloomedlotus.com.

DEDICATION

This book is dedicated to Mother, my first teacher, to every teacher that followed—each in their own unique disguises, and to all that are on the path of self-discovery.

CONTENTS

Introduction		ix
PART 1: UNCOVERING		**1**
CHAPTER 1	The Beginning of Transformation	3
CHAPTER 2	A Dream for Awakening	10
CHAPTER 3	Redefining Duty	17
CHAPTER 4	Meeting the Girl in Red	23
PART 2: UNDERSTANDING		**33**
CHAPTER 5	Mapping the Journey with Help from the Three Little Pigs	35
CHAPTER 6	Dismantling the House of Sticks	43
CHAPTER 7	On the Trail of the Wolf	51
CHAPTER 8	Acceptance—the Foundation for a House of Bricks	55
CHAPTER 9	Guilty until Proven Responsible	61

PART 3: LESSONS AND LEARNING — 73

CHAPTER 10   Teachings for a New Consciousness   75

CHAPTER 11   On My Own   85

CHAPTER 12   Fear, the First Responder   93

CHAPTER 13   Seven and a Half Years to Surrender   101

PART 4: DEEPENING — 113

CHAPTER 14   Interbeing in the World Wide Web   115

CHAPTER 15   Learning of the Emotional Triangle   123

CHAPTER 16   Grounding in Groundlessness   132

CHAPTER 17   A New Old Relationship   142

CHAPTER 18   A Pause for Celebration   151

PART 5: ONE-ING — 159

CHAPTER 19   Uplifting Downfalls in the Holy Land   161

CHAPTER 20   The Virtue of Self-Care   170

CHAPTER 21   Another Pilgrimage   175

CHAPTER 22   Coming Full Triangle   184

Epilogue   196

Bonus   198

Acknowledgments   199

About the Author   201

INTRODUCTION

ONE DAY, AS A teenager in India, I had been watching a television program showing different poets reading their work in Hindi. One woman had read her verses, titled "Boxes of Pain." She shared that over time, many women become boxes of pain from the hurt they gather all through their life. Vowing that I would never let myself become one of them, I decided to be a box of joy and positivity instead. So I made a checklist of things I was going to do to get there and live happily ever after.

My response was not unusual. In fact, both scientists and seers observe that human beings are wired to pursue pleasure and avoid pain. We go to great lengths to control life and play it safe. Yet pain has its own gifts, and Mother Nature has her own way of making sure those gifts are served to us. And if we are wise, we will open up to receive them.

As much as I wanted to be happy, my struggles with pain began in my forties. Starting with a mild restlessness, it grew over the next months into worry, shifted into obsessive thoughts, and was followed by a deep, ongoing hopelessness.

Raised in India with barely any education about mental health, I did not understand what was unfolding in me. Also, I had just started my meditation and self-awareness studio, Full Bloomed Lotus, and had moved my small meditation and discussion groups out of my home and into a rented space, hoping to expand my audience. So, day after day, I followed what I believed was the right choice—repressing negative emotions, going out into the world, and doing what needed to be done.

It was Carl Jung, the Swiss thinker and psychoanalyst, who said, "Your destiny awaits you in the paths you take to avoid it." And so it was that the more I turned away, the more I ended up with the pain I wanted to escape. Months passed this way. And just when I thought I would never find joy again, I had a breakthrough. The key to my healing was revealed in a dream that exposed the disconnect between my adult self and my inner child, who had been previously unknown to me. At the culmination of the dream, that child and I were reunited, and I experienced the joy of wholeness for the first time in my life.

Inspired by the dream, I delved into my childhood, uncovering stories in need of closure and pain in need of release. Applying insights from spiritual teachings and using my imagination, I forged a healing path, coming up with many different exercises that I used to rewire my thinking and emotions to integrate my inner child—my original self. This also helped me individuate from my powerful mother, whose fierce love had kept me from finding myself.

The inner child is our essence, a drop of the divine, and the way nature created us to be. The inner adult—our ego—is our personal manager, who negotiates the world outside. Over a lifetime, by internalizing our failures or peoples' judgments of us or by comparing ourselves to others, the inner adult unconsciously wounds and rejects this deeper, truer self.

When we do inner-child work, we're healing and reclaiming the hurt and neglected parts of ourselves. This is not to say that everything about our natural self is perfect. Like all things in nature, such as rivers and mountains, human beings were created with potential, not perfection. And just like we build dams to conserve and redirect the water or dig tunnels to make pathways, the role of the inner adult is to understand and appreciate our primary natural resource—ourselves—and work with it to channel our light, intentionally and powerfully.

Continuing on this path of self-discovery, I met many others, both women and men, whose stories were different from mine but whose struggles were essentially the same. We were all in the midst of transitioning from the first half of life—when we are led by our conditioning, upbringing, and external environments—to the second half—when we are led by our soul to become the person we were always meant to be.

The challenges of the midlife transition are universal and among the world's best-kept secrets. Most of us are unprepared for the seismic changes that await us in our forties, fifties, and beyond. Our hormonal makeup changes, relationships evolve, marriages lose their freshness, children step into adolescence, parents enter the final leg of their life journey, and our own bodies gradually begin to age. These stages are unavoidable, and they are not the problem per se. When they occur upon an inner psychic structure that has already been weakened by the wounds inflicted by nature and nurture in the first half of life, they cause the entire system to weaken. We feel fragile, yet we try to power through the way we always have. We break open as a result. It comes as no surprise that, as per the CDC's 2021 statistics, adults aged thirty-five to sixty-four account for almost half of all suicides in the US.[1]

Yet, we are not the first people on Earth to feel this angst. Spiritual teachers and thinkers have already walked this journey and left us the breadcrumbs of their teachings. When we navigate these transitions with the deep wisdom of the ages, unlearning old beliefs and cultivating a deeper understanding of the truth, we arrive at a life far more meaningful and real than ever before.

The happily-ever-after we were promised in youth is possible, but not from the world outside alone. Pleasures from earthly experiences, while being

---

[1] https://emedicine.medscape.com/article/2013085-overview?form=fpff

enjoyable, are not permanent, whereas the world within is rich with treasures that bring about abiding joy.

As I experienced fulfillment from my own transformation, I began sharing my understanding and methodologies with others on the journey, guiding them to heal and integrate their deeper identity—their inner child—into a new sense of self. I witnessed their transformation as they made their way into the second half of their lives in alignment with their true nature.

Encouraged by these successes, I offer this book so these teachings can reach a wider audience and help others navigate the emotional peaks and valleys of the midlife years and after. I wrote *The Yoga of Self-Love* as a memoir to share relatable anecdotes, inviting you to walk alongside me rather than as a one-size-fits-all prescriptive approach. Each chapter concludes with reflections and exercises that provide tools to guide you on your own journey toward wholeness and self-love.

As Dr. Deepak Chopra said, "Joy is a return to the deep harmony of body, mind, and spirit that was yours at birth and that can be yours again. That openness to love, that capacity for wholeness with the world around you, is still within you." May this book and its wisdom help you heal and embrace your precious and sacred inner child and return you to the joy and wholeness that is yours to claim. May it empower you to play the unique role that only your authentic self can play in this world, no matter where you are in your life.

PART 1

UNCOVERING

CHAPTER 1

THE BEGINNING OF TRANSFORMATION

EVERY SUMMER, MY HUSBAND, children, and I left our home in Illinois to visit our extended family in India, most of whom lived in the southern city of Bengaluru. One such summer found me visiting my spiritual teacher, Guruji, as his students addressed him. *Guru* means "teacher," and *ji* is a respectful suffix. He was a retired mathematics professor, but his life now centered around teaching Yoga.

I knew Guruji through my sister, Usha, who lives in India. We were three siblings—my brother, Ravi, being the oldest and me being the last. Usha and I were committed to a spiritual journey. We frequently crossed paths, sharing teachings and teachers with one another.

Usha had met Guruji some ten years earlier, and he had initiated her into Kundalini Yoga, an ancient practice of worshiping the divine feminine. The worship combined Yoga postures, breathwork, visualization, chanting, and meditation. Profoundly impacted by the practice, Usha had taught it to me, thus indirectly making me a student of Guruji. After that, my annual visits to Bengaluru included a one-on-one meeting with Guruji.

Each visit was like an annual checkup with a physician, except it was an evaluation of where I was energetically. Guruji had a gift cultivated through years of Yogic practices. His intuitive eye measured an individual's internal well-being beyond their own awareness. And just like a physician might prescribe supplements at the end of a checkup, Guruji would prescribe something—a breathing exercise, a posture, a chant, or a combination of them all—to shift the internal climate and take the person farther along on their journey.

We met in his classroom, above the main house where Guruji lived with his family. This room had no furniture, just a large bamboo mat for students to sit on and a wooden plank that served as his seat. He was in his seventies but looked much younger, his body lean and his face shining with a glow from a healthy lifestyle and Yogic practices.

It was a pleasant afternoon, with the sunlight pouring through a large window on one side of the room. It had rained earlier in the day, but the clouds had cleared. The rainy season in Bengaluru has this unique way of showering the earth with a heavy downpour and then following it up with a much-mellowed sun, golden and warm and not too bright—a quality I had grown to love. Although I was raised in Mumbai, our extended family lived in Bengaluru, and my annual summer visits to this city began when I was a child.

Our session lasted over an hour, with Guruji giving me his usual guidance. We were wrapping up our visit when a serious expression came over his face.

"Ramaa," he said. "I see that you are soon to start a difficult chapter in your life and meet with many challenging situations."

I had long believed in Guruji's intuitive gifts and capacity to see more than meets the physical eye. But never before had he offered a prediction for my future—or one this ominous. My heart sank while my mind began frantically searching for a way to circumvent the difficult times he was portending. I remembered reading that the grace of a guru could protect one from any disaster. Sitting up with a new hope, I appealed to him to change my fate.

Folding my palms together in a namaste, I said, "Guruji, you are a powerful master. Please make whatever it is go away with your miraculous powers."

He smiled and said, "It doesn't work that way. This is the journey your soul planned, and no one, not even a teacher, has the right to take that away from you. Face your life fearlessly and keep guilt at bay. Find meaning and grow through all your struggles."

I took a deep breath and nodded slowly, little knowing how often I would replay his words of advice in the coming years.

A few weeks later, my family and I returned to our home in Chicago. Fall came, schools started up again, and we all returned to our normal routines.

* * *

The months unfolded into a difficult year. I had been teaching meditation and self-awareness practices in small groups at my home for a few years. Encouraged by many within our community and wanting to expand my audience, I had recently ventured out and rented a studio space. It turned out that running a business was more difficult than I had realized. The expansion I had expected was not happening, while many unanticipated problems were coming up. Several ideas with initial momentum were no longer working.

Things at home were also changing. My husband, Krish, and I have two children—first a son, whom we'd named Anish, and then a daughter, Amrita. Our son was born in India, where we had been living with Krish's parents and extended family, all under the same roof, as is the practice there. Shortly before Anish turned two, we left India for Thailand to pursue career opportunities. After a couple of years there, a new work project had us packing up again to leave for Israel, where we lived for close to a year before returning to Thailand. Six months after that, our family was once again on the move, this time to Chicago. Our travels meant our firstborn went to three different preschools—two in Thailand and one in Israel. He was just over five years old when we arrived in Chicago, expecting our second child, his sister.

We settled into our new life, experiencing the usual ups and downs that come with parenthood. Now, however, something worrisome was going on. Our teenage son, usually a bright student, was not doing well in his high school classes. At home, he had become more and more sullen and withdrawn. At school, his grades were falling at a time when they were starting to matter. He would be the first in our family to enter college in America, and I was keen on getting this right. Unable to understand what was going on, I worried about him and his future every day.

Around this same time, Krish's position at work had shifted with a recent promotion that required him to travel frequently. This meant that, more often than not, I was left to play "bad cop" in our parenting roles. Anish grew distant from me, and the distance felt like a rejection. It weighed heavily upon my heart.

Meanwhile, in India, my father suffered a second stroke, fifteen years after his first, and my mother's cancer returned after an eight-year reprieve.

My confidence in life grew shaky, and I found myself becoming increasingly downcast. Tears came often, and nothing seemed to bring me joy.

When I was with friends, all I could focus on was how much better their lives were than mine or how well their children were doing while my son was struggling. It was painful to be with company, and I soon lost all interest in having a social life, keeping to my work and my family.

In years past, I had sought advice from my mother, who had always been my hero. We had established a routine of catching up each weekend, and I would share with her anything that was bothering me. Down to earth and practical, she seemed to have the perfect solution for every situation. But this time, nothing Mother said could stop my downward spiral. She did try, in her usual matter-of-fact way. "Get yourself in check," she would say. "No matter what happens, be brave and keep the faith! Look at me. I am facing my cancer fearlessly."

Her words fell on deaf ears, as each time, I hung up the phone and returned to my unhappy state of mind. I didn't have the positivity in me to pick myself up the way she told me to, and I spent sleepless nights worried that my optimism had left me forever.

I looked for strength through my spiritual practice. My daily routine of Kundalini Yoga gave me a respite, no doubt, but it was like taking a painkiller. After a few hours of relief, the deep, unnameable sadness would return.

My sister, Usha, was a teacher and spiritual counselor in India, and I would often call her as well, seeking solace. One morning, I learned that Anu, a neighbor and one of my few friends, was relocating to a new city. In my fragile state of mind, it felt like a calamity. I called Usha right away, seeking her strength. She answered the phone in her usual cheerful voice and listened patiently as I broke down, sharing my bad news of the day.

When I had calmed down, she said, "You've been crying a lot lately. And don't get me wrong, but these are not big problems. I was just speaking to a woman who lost her child to cancer. There are people out there dealing with real tragedies. You have a blessed life—a caring husband, a nice family, and good health. Many people would love to walk in your shoes right now."

I was silent. What does one say to that?

"You need to change your approach to life," she continued. "Start a gratitude journal. Each day, look around you and list five things you are grateful for. It will change your life, I assure you."

It sounded like a great idea. I promised her I would start the practice. The next morning, I woke up with the same sinking feeling in my heart, but true to my word, I listed five things I was grateful for. However, the exercise did not lift my spirits. The pain arose from a far deeper place in me, and the gratitude felt like a cover-up, a bandage that brought no relief. After attempting the gratitude exercise for a few more days, I gave it up altogether and felt worse for having failed.

* * *

A few days later, I shared my woes during my annual visit with Cathie Dunal, my physician and friend. She looked at me for a long moment before gently suggesting that I consider taking an antidepressant. The medication would "take the edge off," she said. I balked at the suggestion. I was wary of Western medicine and its side effects[2], and I wanted to go there only if things got really, really bad. Surely, I wasn't there yet?

Cathie looked worried. With concern in her voice, she insisted I return in a few weeks should there be no change. Her serious expression was one I had never seen before. It woke me up; my sadness was not just going to disappear on its own the way I had imagined. It needed intervention, although I did not know what that might be. I told Cathie I needed time to figure this out for myself, then I left, promising to reach out to her should things get worse.

Driving away from that visit, I felt sorry for myself. All my life, I had tried to be positive in my thinking and worked hard to be a force for good in the community. I had even started a center for self-awareness to teach people how to manage their thoughts. Ironically, I had helped people get off antidepressants and boost themselves up through meditation and breathwork. Yet there I was, struggling in my own life. Things with my family and my business were challenging, and I was overwhelmed by it all.

Another worry was beginning to surface. I had been practicing Kundalini Yoga diligently for more than eight years. The books I had read described practitioners having visions of light and visitations from angels. I had been

---

2   Such was my thinking at the time. I now know that medication can give someone much needed reprieve from certain conditions, enough space even to do the inner work needed for further healing. I regularly ask people to consult a professional on whether medical intervention could help. I was also raised to believe that therapy was for the weak and unstable—another notion I have since dismissed. I now strongly recommend therapy as a path for those who need a guide for their inner work.

secretly waiting and hoping for such a reward myself. Instead, my life was beset with problems. Could it be that I was not doing the practice right and was, therefore, being punished by the Goddess? I wondered if I needed to call Guruji and share my concerns with him.

It was then that I remembered my conversation with him ten months earlier. In the busyness of my life, Guruji's predictions had slipped my mind entirely! He had said there were difficult times ahead.

"Face your life fearlessly and keep guilt at bay." His words came back to me, as did his sense that my challenges were the journey my soul had chosen for growth. Some comfort came from the memory, particularly his advice to leave guilt out of my interpretations. Whatever my challenges, they were my destiny, and I had to keep moving forward.

Getting home from Cathie's, I headed to a quiet corner and sat down to pray. Usually, I prayed for my mother, my father, my children, and my community, but that day, I prayed for me—for the clarity to understand what I needed to do and the strength to find relief from my suffering.

CHAPTER REFLECTIONS

1. Have you experienced prolonged periods of sadness? When were they? And what was going on in your life at the time?

2. What remedies did you explore? Which worked?

3. Things began to shift for me when I allowed myself to pray for my own well-being. What can you do to be open to receiving help when you think you've reached a dead end?

CHAPTER 2

A DREAM FOR AWAKENING

AS I STRUGGLED, TRYING to find answers to my questions, I began having vivid dreams each night of places and people I did not recognize. On some nights, the dreams were full of colorful trees and strange creatures unlike any I had seen in real life. They made no sense to me, so I attributed this unusual phenomenon to the stress I was experiencing in my waking hours.

Then I met Jackie Walker.

After teaching a class one morning, I walked to the front of the studio and saw a woman I hadn't met before. Of medium height, slim and dark haired, she was standing by a little shelf in the reception area where I had stacked an assortment of books for sale. I immediately noticed the book she was reading: Ruth Montgomery's *A Search for the Truth*. It was one of my earliest inspirations. With the words closely crammed into its pages, the book looked unappealing. That was probably the reason I had failed, despite my frequent attempts, to get my students to read it. Seeing she had picked up that book, I felt an immediate warmth toward her.

One of the ladies from my class greeted the woman. As I approached them, the woman from my class addressed me.

"Ramaa, I want to introduce you to my friend, Jackie Walker. You'd be so interested in her work." She started to rave about Jackie's talents as a tarot card reader and dream interpreter. Given my recent dreams, I was intrigued.

"Dream interpretation? That's interesting. I've been dreaming a lot lately, but I thought it was just my mind on overdrive," I said, half joking.

"It's more than that," Jackie said. "It is your mind giving you messages from your unconscious."

"I see . . . I guess some dreams are messages, but mine just make no sense," I replied.

"Every dream is a message," Jackie corrected. "Some are just more clear-cut than others. That is why they need interpretation."

I wanted to know more and realized the subject called for a longer conversation, so I decided to make an appointment to meet with her privately.

* * *

Eager to share some of my recent dreams, I couldn't wait for my meeting with Jackie. But the night before the appointment, I had a dream so powerful that all the others faded into the background.

In my dream, I saw myself descending in an elevator on top of a hill. I was draped in a white sari, and along with me was a little girl, about five years old, wearing a red dress (a frock, as we called it in the old days in India).

We stepped off the elevator to find ourselves at the top of a long flight of stairs winding down the hill. I turned my back to the stairs and sat at the top, reading a financial weekly, while the little girl continued down the stairs. Very soon, I heard her loud cries. Looking over my shoulder and seeing that she had fallen, I tossed the magazine aside and rushed to her. Getting on my knees at eye level with her, I gathered her into a close embrace. The moment we connected, my heart filled with love and joy in a way I had never experienced in my waking hours. Then the dream ended.

I woke up, my heart racing, my face wet with tears. It was still too early to get up, but I couldn't fall back asleep. The exhilaration from my dream left my heart aglow even as the tremendous sadness of the wounded girl cast a shadow. A bright, surreal light had surrounded the entire dream.

Delving into dream interpretation in the coming years, I came to know this as a "big dream." And I learned that there is a word for the energy around it—*numinosity*. It is derived from the Latin word *numen*, which means "something filled with a sense of a mysterious presence or divinity."

But that morning, all I knew was the emotional state the dream had left me in, with waves of joy and sadness rising up from time to time. Even more eager to meet with Jackie now, I wondered who the girl was and tried to remember if I had known her from my life in the US or earlier in India.

* * *

Finally, I arrived at Jackie's apartment. We sat down, and I shared my dream. Jackie wanted me to describe every detail as she listened quietly and took notes. Then it was her turn to speak.

"Dreams are messages from our unconscious," she reminded me. "We all have parts of our life that we are unaware of. Dreams seek to correct that and give us clues that can help us with the situations we're struggling with in our waking world."

"I have been practicing self-awareness for years now. How could I be unaware?" I wondered aloud, thinking back to the practice of mindfulness that I had woven into my everyday activities.

"You are no doubt aware of many things but not everything," Jackie explained. "As humans, we are conditioned early on in life to pay attention selectively. Some of us may focus on work, some of us on beauty or perfection, and so on. Whatever we fail to pay attention to recedes into the unconscious and causes problems in our lives. Dreams reveal what they are."

"Like a side mirror that shows us what's not in front of us?" I asked.

"Yes, you could say that," Jackie said as she built on the analogy. "And just as those side mirrors can prevent accidents, analyzing your dreams can help you avoid difficult situations in your life."

I nodded, trying to understand what she was telling me, and looked around the room. One wall was covered with shelves thickly packed with books. Jackie had decorated the room with colorful images of angels and gorgeous gemstones.

She went on to analyze my dream.

"First off, all the characters in a dream are aspects of one's own self. While you identify with the woman in the sari, that girl in red is also you. The woman represents the adult you are, while the child is your younger, playful self."

This was fascinating to me because I had thought we grow up and leave our younger selves behind. That a younger version of me still lived within was news to me. Taking it all in, I imagined life unfolding like a movie, with the scenes and actors changing but leaving behind the old reels of memory intact.

As we continued, Jackie explained that the dream revealed how my adult self and my inner child had begun our journey together. But somewhere along the way, I had let go of her and turned my attention to whatever it was I was reading.

"I was reading a financial magazine, but I never read them in reality. For that matter, I seldom wear a sari these days," I offered.

"Dreams are not to be interpreted literally. You need to see them with a metaphoric lens." Seeing my puzzled expression, Jackie continued. "The details in your dream are symbols and need to be understood as such. For example, your dream could be saying that you ignored the child in you because you were focused on your financial concerns. The sari may represent traditional values that you are wrapped up in. Does that ring true?"

"Wow, that's brilliant, and yes, it does ring true!" I said. "These past months since starting my studio have been rough. I have been trying to pay my rent and make ends meet without asking my husband for help. A lot has been going on within my family as well, and I have been busy juggling many balls."

"I understand. And the one you dropped was that little girl who has been hurt and is now crying to get your attention."

"Are you saying it is the pain of my younger self that has been tugging at me these past months, and not the other unfortunate events of my life?" I asked.

She paused thoughtfully before replying.

"I would say that all the problems in your life are causing some unhappiness, for sure, but the added intensity of your emotions is owing to the wounds of your inner child. Dreams reveal the reasons for the sadness that you are not in touch with. The good news is that the same dream is also offering you a way out of the pain. When you reunite with your inner child, you will find great joy, and that will help you handle the outer challenges of your life with fortitude."

Her words brought to mind Guruji's advice once more, and I made a note to reflect later on how it might be connected to my dream. Right now, Jackie was pulling a book from her vast library. I listened, hanging on every word as she read to me about the vulnerable inner child being a powerful energy within us that draws in the people and events needed to heal its wounds.

I was wide-eyed with wonder as a thought suddenly occurred to me.

"Jackie!" I exclaimed. "Meeting you at my studio was no accident. You were part of my inner child's plan!"

"Definitely," she said. "Things do unfold in accordance with a deeper plan. And there could be many more people coming your way, so keep your eyes open."

Her assurance lifted my spirits. Just as Jackie had walked into my life with all this wisdom, others would help show me the way. I felt a wave of relief that I would not be left alone to figure out how to heal my hidden wounds.

As our appointment came to an end, Jackie asked me to continue revisiting the dream and journal about it.

"Dreams have hidden layers of meaning," she said. "You need to revisit it often and look at it from many angles. Remember, every detail is a piece of the puzzle. And only you know how it fits in."

She suggested I keep a dream journal and track my dreams, even if it meant waking up at night to do so. I promised I would do my best, then prepared to leave. At the door, I gave her a big hug and thanked her profusely.

"Do come back if you have more dreams you need to work through" were her parting words.

Leaving, I knew there was a lot to unpack. This felt big. *What do I need to do?* I wondered. *Do I call and speak to Mother? Or ask Usha for next steps?*

Raised as the youngest child, I had always needed the validation of those older in the family, particularly Mother and Usha. Although a wife and a mother myself, I still relied on them for guidance and direction when it came to important decisions. In fact, one of my recent frustrations had been their inability to help me.

I checked the clock to see what time it was in India. Then my mind turned to Guruji's words. He had said this was my journey, that I had to find meaning and grow through it all. That advice was making more sense to me now. Perhaps the dream and its message were my opportunity to finally grow up.

The rest of the day went by with my usual chores and responsibilities. As I settled in for the night, my mind was still buzzing with thoughts and questions from my time with Jackie.

Does everyone have an inner child, and are they all connected to theirs? When did I part from mine? And why did my adult self, who has overcome many challenges and helped so many others, turn her back on the child within? What does it mean to "go down and embrace" her?

I did not have the answers to my questions, but the delicious feeling from my dream still burned brightly and lit up my heart. That was enough for now.

CHAPTER REFLECTIONS

1. Dreams are a great resource for revealing our blind spots. Consider maintaining a dream journal by your bedside.

2. Before turning in for the day, let go of your worries and ask your subconscious mind to show you the way out through your dreams. If you have a dream that feels significant, note it in your dream journal and use Jackie's advice to decode the message. Be patient as you do this each night. It may take a few days or weeks for the dream to show up. Keep an eye out for themes.

3. Is there some aspect of your life that you have repressed or denied?

CHAPTER 3

REDEFINING DUTY

INSIGHT #1

Right action is a personal choice and responsibility.

I BEGAN THE NEXT PHASE of this journey after my meeting with Jackie. She had asked me to revisit the big dream regularly and, using my memories and imagination, connect with the little girl and journal about everything I uncovered. Inspired by her words and being ever the good student, I was committed to my assignment. With the excitement of someone starting a new school year, I bought myself a beautiful new journal and a set of fine-tip pens.

That was the easy part. Actually finding time to journal was the tough part. Given my routine, tossing aside my commitments and rushing down to embrace my inner child was easier said than done. My life was busy, and I had lots of responsibilities.

I went through my calendar to look for an opening but found none. My day began in the wee hours at four thirty with my Kundalini practice, which was made of several segments that lasted over ninety minutes. After that, my duties as a mother, cook, and chauffeur took over. After dropping my children at school, I headed for the studio to teach or prepare for my classes, then returned just in time to pick up the children. The rest of the day was busy with other chores, including cooking a healthy dinner, cleaning up, and supervising homework. I was spent by the time I retired to bed at ten. On weekends, our children had their activities and assignments, which needed close monitoring. Everything in my day seemed necessary and important.

Over a week went by, and, uncomfortable with dropping any single activity, I had not touched the new journal. I examined my reluctance to make changes to the routine. Figuring out where my rigidity came from was a no-brainer, as I had been raised by a very strong and disciplined mother whose every hour could be accounted for with some productive activity. She ran a very organized household, was great at her work, and cooked up wonders in the kitchen.

"Do not waste your time, and never fail in your duty," Mother often said to my siblings and me, leading by example. "At the end of the day, that is what God asks each one of us. 'Have you done your duty?'"

I imagined God receiving us upon death with a checklist and did not dare think of what might happen if the answer to that question was, "No, not really." I suspect Mother hadn't gone that far in her own imagination either.

Mother quoted her source for this advice as the *Bhagavad Gita* (meaning "song of God"), the sacred book for the Hindus. The word for "duty" is *dharma*, which is interpreted to mean "one's obligations toward their religion, family, parents, neighbors, the poor, the needy, one's community, and one's country." Never one's own self. Helping others is more important than self-care, which is seen as selfish. Giving is better than receiving.

Those are the values I was raised with, and although I had largely left the *Bhagavad Gita* behind and was living thousands of miles away, I still held those values. I followed Mother's cues faithfully, filling my day with "productive" activities. I feared failing in any of the duties on my dharma list of obligations. An hour of journaling and connecting with that little girl of my dreams felt like an unholy indulgence or, in Mother's words, "a waste of precious time."

Looking at my planner again, I saw that my only real undisturbed time were the predawn hours when the rest of the family was still sleeping. But that slot was already taken. For eight years, I had dedicated my early mornings to Kundalini Yoga and held this daily dedication to the Goddess as sacred and nonnegotiable. It was the traditional path, followed by the many teachers I had admired and read about: the postures, the chants, the breathwork. I was reluctant to put them, or any part of them, aside to explore this relationship with the girl I had met in my dreams.

I had not anticipated this conflict during my session with Jackie. Her wisdom and my dream had both felt so right that I had heartily agreed to her advice. But now I was torn between my old routine and this new path, and I wished for a resolution to the dilemma of what the right course of action was.

A few days later, my wish was granted.

I was having coffee with my dear friend Maren. Her birthday was coming up, and I asked her if there was anything on her wish list I could give her.

"Yes, thanks for asking. There is!" she said. Then she went on to ask, "Have you read the *Gita*?"

I hesitated, reluctant to share my sentiments. My relationship with the *Bhagavad Gita*, or simply *Gita* as it is known, was a troubled one. On the one hand, I was raised to believe it is the word of God and regarded it with respect. On the other, reading it as a teenager, I had come upon its references to the caste system that plagues India, and struggled to understand how a God who was supposed to be fair could have come up with an order that does not treat all beings as equal. Unable to resolve the discord, I had turned away from the holy book.

"Yes, I have. Why do you ask?" I ventured cautiously.

"I just keep finding references to the *Gita* in different places and want to read it. Like with the Bible, I am sure there are many translations. Could you pick out the right one for me? I would trust your choice."

"I'd love to," I replied, despite my discomfort.

At the bookstore the next day, it became clear very soon why Maren needed my help. There were nearly fifteen translations with varying levels of commentaries. I found a comfortable spot and sat down to look for one that would help a new reader coming from the West. Many of the translations were religious in their approach. Their language was familiar to me, but I needed a universal perspective. Eventually, I opened a translation by Stephen Mitchell. Just reading the introduction, I knew I'd found what I was looking for. Mitchell had approached the work as a seeker of wisdom and not as a Hindu per se. I flipped through the book, randomly opening a page. My eyes fell on these words: "It is better to do your own duty badly, than to perfectly do another's."

Goosebumps.

Given my recent internal debates over the question of duty, this was serendipitous. The words were exactly what I needed. I closed the book and decided that the *Gita* was inviting me to read it again, with a new translation this time. I bought a copy for Maren and one for myself, then started over the same day.

Revisiting the *Gita* thirty years after I last read it meant I would read and understand it differently. In those thirty years, I had grown into an adult, completed my education, left India, traveled to many countries, and explored other faiths. Reviewing the words with this broadened lens and with help from a translation that was universal, I was beginning a new relationship with an ancient text that would soon become my guide.

The *Gita*, like most Hindu scriptures, was originally written in the classical Sanskrit. Since only a small percentage of people even in India still know the language, it has been translated into all the local dialects.

I returned to my copy to reflect on the words that had jumped out at me in the bookstore: "It is better to do your own duty badly, than to perfectly do another's."

As described above, dharma is generally understood to mean "right action" or "responsibility," as determined at birth simply and only by the caste of the family one was born into. But with my recent dream of the inner child, I was beginning to wonder if the word was meant to also take into consideration one's emotions, talents, and personal ethics.

With this viewpoint, even the *Gita*'s chapter on the four castes made sense. I had originally struggled with the idea of a hierarchical social order based on one's birth, which was how the caste system had been explained to me. It had seemed unfair. But if one interprets dharma as "aligning with one's inner nature," then the *Gita* is grouping people in accordance with their predispositions and directing them to follow their inborn strengths, which is brilliant!

For years, I had adhered to a cherished outer practice that I had been initiated into. But now I felt deeply called to look within and address the pain of my inner child. The words from the *Gita* felt like the divine endorsement I had been waiting for.

The verse about dharma was followed by another line: "You are safe from harm when you do what you should be doing."

The Universe was sending me a message.

Can I trust the God I believe in? I wondered.

I pondered the question for a couple more days before clarity dawned.

Right action, or dharma, is a personal choice and responsibility. Our needs change over time, and we owe it to ourselves to recognize the internal shifts and redefine dharma based on who we are now.

Only by looking deeply and connecting with the unhappy child within would I know my next steps. That was my foremost dharma and sacred duty to myself.

So I created a new morning routine. My day would begin with my inner work. I would then follow it up with an abridged version of my Kundalini practice.

That felt right. My journey was now ready for launch.

CHAPTER REFLECTIONS

1. Setting aside time for your inner work each day is as important as eating healthy or exercising regularly. Do you believe one-on-one time with yourself is selfish or unproductive?

2. Take a look at your calendar, and create a window of time to slow down, reflect, and send love to yourself. Start small, doing this for just ten minutes a day at first, then expand it over time.

3. If you need to give up some sleep to make time for yourself, know that the energy you will receive from your inner work will more than make up for the lost sleep.

CHAPTER 4

MEETING THE GIRL IN RED

INSIGHT #2
*You can't change the past, but love supplements
can rejuvenate you in the present.*

THE WORDS IN THE *Gita* empowered me to follow my own dharma. I felt I had received permission to embark on this path of self-exploration and opened myself up to what I might learn from the experience. The only problem was that I had no external teacher giving me instructions for every step of this unorthodox expedition.

Jackie, the dream interpreter, had said my dream was a message from my unconscious asking me to reconnect with my wounded inner child. But she hadn't told me how to do that or what those wounds might be. It was up to me to figure it out. I was again reminded of Guruji's words that this was my journey to take.

So I sat comfortably on the couch in our living room, my journal next to me, and wondered how to get started. I remembered Jackie saying that every detail of the dream was a symbol I should take a closer look at. By journaling about my associations with each detail, I could understand the message even more deeply. The images in the dream were still vivid in my mind, so I decided to start by drawing the scene in my sketchbook and filling it up with colors.

Although I'm not a great artist, the picture was a fairly good representation of my dream. I gazed at it for a while, waiting to see what caught my attention.

The first thing that spoke to me was the stark color difference between what the two versions of myself wore. My adult self was draped in a white sari while the child me was dressed in vibrant red. I began by writing down my associations with each color. White is the color of purity and wisdom; red feels like earthiness. I toyed with an interpretation that my adult self was immersed in spirituality while my younger self was clothed in earthly aspirations.

Then there was the staircase that separated us. *What does that mean?* I wondered. *Is the staircase indicating a hierarchy in the values between my two selves? Could that be the reason for the split between them?*

Reflecting on those questions brought about the realization that I had, in fact, embraced a hierarchical value system. Perfection, success, and giving back were good and lofty virtues. Imperfection, failure, and self-indulgence were bad and relegated to the bottom.

This value system came from the tradition I was raised in. Our mythology is filled with stories of gods on the one hand and demons on the other, with the two sides constantly battling for power. I had heard these battles interpreted in Sunday religion classes as our good thoughts and inclinations fighting with our "base" emotions of anger, envy, laziness, and so on. To support the gods, we had to denounce these weak emotions and conquer them—or, at the very least, walk away from them.

I had chosen to distance myself from my weaker side, and that neglected self was now calling for my attention.

My adult self needed to step down, get on her knees, and look deeply at those emotions instead of judging and turning away. It was a scary assignment. The emotions I had repressed made me uncomfortable. And I could sense they were strong too. There was a reason I worked so hard at being "good"! Yet the only way to achieve the beautiful union I longed for was to uncover my demons and face them.

I had to do this for myself.

Starting a new page in my journal, I wrote these words: "This pain is mine. Healing it is not anyone's responsibility but my own."

Then my time for that morning's reflection was up. I put aside my journal and began my regular practice of Kundalini Yoga.

* * *

The next morning, I already had a plan. Thinking about bridging the gap between my adult spiritual self and my earthly inner child, I decided I would begin by writing that girl a letter. I had always been great at writing letters to family and friends, sending notes for no reason at all. Now it was time to turn that effort and kindness toward myself. I wrote:

Dear Little Girl in Red,

I want to begin by saying thank you. Thank you for showing up in my dream. Thank you for sharing your pain with me. Thank you for bringing Jackie into my world so that I could receive your message.

I apologize for not staying in touch with you, for turning away from you and for not being aware of the pain that you have been in. I know you have been there waiting for me to look at you, and I am here now. I will be here for you. Always.

Please talk to me, tell me anything you want me to know, in any ways you can. Let me know what you need from me, and how I can heal you. I am ready to listen and ready to feel uncomfortable. So please share with me what you want me to know.

I will be here again tomorrow and every morning. Just for you.

R

Even as I wrote the letter in my journal, a skeptical and familiar voice kept dismissing the entire exercise, whispering that I was being silly and "wasting precious time." I recognized that voice. It was the voice that was desperate to keep me tied to my old ways—the ways that told me making a productive choice was better than doing something unpredictable.

I chose to ignore the voice and move on, thus taking my first step down that staircase.

After that, it was easier. When I finished my letter-writing exercise, I visualized embracing the little girl and wished I had a picture of myself at that age. But the few that had been taken at the time were at my parents' home in India. I wrapped my arms around my tummy, imagining she was sitting on my lap. I visualized her face as I remembered photographs from my childhood. She was looking up at me with her sad little face and big brown eyes. Stroking her hair, I whispered loving words in her ears and held her close. It seemed like a part of me had come home for the first time, and I felt whole as we sat quietly and breathed together. There were no words between us.

Waves of peace and joy swept over me. I had been meditating for years using my mantra and other breathing techniques, but none of them had brought me to this place. It was as if I had unearthed the most troublesome part of my mind and quieted it with my loving attention. It felt deep and spiritual, and I decided this would be my new meditation practice.

Every morning after that, I began my inner work by calling forth the little girl in red. Imagining her seated on my lap and drawing her close, I would quietly assure her that everything was going to be all right. We would breathe as one, and it would put me into a peaceful state, where I would remain for as much time as I could afford that day. The sense of comfort that came from holding that little girl stayed with me for several hours after. No deity I had ever worshiped felt so close or evoked so much love in me.

* * *

I was settling into my new routine, and it felt good. I still wanted to know what wounds the little girl was carrying that I needed to address. Since I did not have any photographs from my childhood, anytime I saw a picture of a little brown girl, I would cut it out, stick it in my journal, and speak to her as if she were me. At bedtime, I would ask her to tell me anything she wanted me to know, and I would reaffirm my commitment to remain by her side no matter what. Just as Jackie had suggested, I kept my journal by my bedside as I prepared for more revelatory dreams. I did not know what to expect. But in a few days, I would—and it would be more than I had bargained for!

I was on a walk when the first of the memories surfaced. It came back with great clarity as though it had happened only a few months earlier.

When we were children, Ravi and Usha went to a school that had Thursdays off each week in addition to the Sunday holiday. The school I went to had a different schedule. The memory was from a Thursday. I had returned home from school to find that Ravi and Usha had decapitated my doll and were in the middle of setting it on fire. The intense pain of the memory rising from the very depths of my past engulfed me. Taken by surprise, I began weeping, much to the concern of a walker on the other side of the street.

A day later, another memory bubbled up. One evening, I had gone to a friend's house to play. Unexpectedly, her mother accused me of something I hadn't done, and her loud voice yelling at me stunned and rooted me to the spot where I was standing. Returning home, I shared the story with Mother, who asked me to go back and "apologize anyway" to make peace with that family.

A few days later, another memory came—this one particularly painful. I had signed up to participate in a group dance at school. For weeks, we practiced every evening at the dance teacher's home. On the day of the final rehearsal at the venue, she realized the stage was too small for so many of us, and I was one of the kids dropped out of the dance. I returned home feeling rejected.

Then there were more memories. Small hurts, bigger hurts. Not only from my five-year-old self but from much later in my life as well, all the way up to my most recent years. I was astounded by these memories and the intensity of the emotions they carried. Having led a relatively uneventful life, I mostly felt fortunate that there had been no big disasters or upheavals. I had no idea that the mundane miseries of an ordinary life could add up to such sizeable baggage.

Certainly, my recent routine of gathering my inner child close and assuring her she could trust my adult self had led to this upsurge. She was inviting me to look at the stories she had filed away and process them for her. And they just kept coming up like undigested food. If I had been my own physician, that would have been my prognosis: emotional indigestion. And just as undigested food can cause ill health, these undigested events and emotions had been causing me so much agony.

At first, I was not sure what I was supposed to do with all these flashbacks. But working with the metaphor of digestion helped me find clarity. Digestion is the act of transforming what we eat into energy and eliminating what is unhealthy or indigestible. When our digestive system is up and running, we are high in energy and able to do great things with our bodies. While physical digestion is involuntary, digesting what lands on the platter of life is a voluntary act. We need to actively choose what we wish to retain and what we need to release.

As I looked back on the memories, I could see what my system had thrown up. I realized that growing up as the youngest of three, I was more sensitive and emotional than the rest of my family. I recalled the many times that I ruminated, grumbled, or whined away in misery while everyone else went about their lives. No one knew what to do with me. Somewhere along the way, I decided it was best to deny and hide those emotions, believing them to be evidence of my weakness. Between the polarities of wallowing and avoiding, there had been no room for the conscious absorption that is digestion. Now my adult self had to attend to each of these unprocessed memories, deciding what to keep and what to let go.

* * *

I began with my first flashback, when my siblings had taken apart my doll. That was ages ago, and our close-knit family had weathered many storms together in the intervening years. It would hardly make sense to go back to them now and lay this memory at their feet. All I could do was feel the pain, let it run its course, and love my inner child through it. I continued to journal my communication with her:

I am so sorry this happened to you. Ravi and Usha are good people. They were having fun without realizing they were hurting you. Children often do hurtful things, and you probably did some awful things to them too. It is okay to let all that go. Leave it be, darling, leave it be!

To help her, I took a deep breath and let out a powerful exhale, then continued with my usual we-breathe-together meditation. In a few minutes, I felt lighter. Sensing she had let go, I was ready to return to my outer life.

Reading the *Gita* daily now, I was understanding health and healing in much deeper ways. True healing not only releases the pressure of the past, but it also builds the inner equanimity and resilience needed to face the challenges in our lives.

My daily routine was now dedicated to picking one or two memories and processing them. Most of them were simply events that could not be changed but needed to be acknowledged, felt, sometimes grieved, and then intentionally released. I kept doing this as best I could. I would write in my journal, offering words to reassure the little girl in red that I had heard her story, felt her pain, and was never going to judge her or let go of her for any reason. At the end of each session, we would embrace, meditate, and start the day together feeling whole and peaceful.

Jackie had told me that integrating inner-child work into my daily routine would also help me deal with my present struggles. Although I had been doubtful, wondering if the whole exercise would be a time drain, I was realizing she was right. By journaling, speaking to my inner child, and working to digest past experiences, I felt a subtle release of tension and a spurt of energy. I realized that my morning session was my emotional supplement, just like a calcium or iron supplement one takes as needed. I could not change the past that had weakened me in some ways, but a daily dose of self-love was renewing me to show up stronger in the present.

I was grateful for my new routine. The journey from woundedness to wisdom was underway.

CHAPTER REFLECTIONS

1. Do you have a favorite photograph from childhood? Create a place for that picture, put it into a frame, or make a collage with it and other favorite images.

2. Speak to your inner child. Offer complete and unconditional love. Imagine drawing that child close and breathing together. Inhaling and exhaling, affirm, "We two are one."

3. What would be your first letter to your inner child? What do you think that child needs to hear you say?

4. Give yourself a daily love supplement in the form of a loving affirmation, such as "I am thankful I am myself," "I am the reason to keep going," or "I love who I am now and believe in who I can be tomorrow."

PART 2

UNDERSTANDING

CHAPTER 5

MAPPING THE JOURNEY WITH HELP FROM THE THREE LITTLE PIGS

INSIGHT #3

*Past storylines return to you in different
forms until they are transformed.*

"PEOPLE WILL FORGET WHAT you said, people will forget what you did, but people will never forget how you made them feel."

So said the great American poet and thinker Maya Angelou. Now experiencing an implosion of old stories, feelings, and conversations, I was realizing the truth of those words. Our bodies remember more than our minds do, locking away unprocessed emotions and impressions, then bringing them to the surface when the time is ripe and asking that they be healed or released.

As I journaled away, the memories kept coming. In most cases, the disappointments of that girl in red seemed so trivial to my adult mind that I was tempted to dismiss them. But having decided that inner work was my dharma, I remained committed to clearing the slate within.

I began to address each incident creatively. Although not an artist, I found myself drawing images from the past or symbols that spoke to me and brought me peace. Writing brought me peace as well. Just writing out the story as I remembered it, then feeling it, helped me set it free.

But sometimes, that little girl needed more in order to let go and move on—an acknowledgment, an apology, forgiveness, or just an assurance that everything was okay. So I decided to step in, writing thank-you notes to my inner child on behalf of someone who had not acknowledged her kindness. Sometimes, I wrote her a note of pardon for something she regretted doing or saying. Other times, I wrote notes of apology from people who had hurt her and would never ask for her forgiveness. Each time, I would write the letter as my present adult self on one day and then read it the following day from my younger self's perspective, feeling the words and breathing them in. And each time, I knew she received it because I felt better.

Thus, my daily sadhana, the traditional word for a spiritual practice, was becoming more and more untraditional. But through all of it, I was also gaining a better understanding of the chakra system that the practice of Kundalini Yoga is founded on.

The chakra system is an ancient body of knowledge. It organizes the human experience around centers of energy aligned along the spine, starting from the base to the crown of the head. There are seven main chakras corresponding to seven groups of nerves, organs, and endocrine systems in the body. The traditional practice of Kundalini Yoga I was initiated into includes breathwork, chanting, visualization, and physical postures intended to animate these seven centers, leading to a healthier and more enlightened way of living. Upon my initiation into the practice, I had read several books by early practitioners and experts. Now, faced with my own experiences, I was coming to understand it all differently.

I began to think of the chakra centers as filing cabinets that store our entire emotional history. While we may think of feelings as simply painful or pleasurable, there are different kinds of pain and pleasure. Hurt, shame, defeat, loss, confusion, worry, and fear, while all being painful, are different from each other in the same way that joy, humor, thrill, optimism, peace, love, and fulfillment have their own places. The mind-body filing system knows these differences and saves the memories of our emotions, each in its own region or cabinet. Our spontaneous reactions are drawn out of this well-organized filing cabinet of memories, moment to moment, even as the system updates with our present experiences.

Keeping detailed notes in my journal as I received more insights, I began noticing that although the characters, times, and places of my memories were different, the themes at their core remained the same.

When I was nine, a dear friend moved away, and I felt lost and sad. Then, when a friend moved out of my neighborhood when I was in my forties, I felt that same sense of bereavement. As a child, performing less than my classmates caused me to feel ashamed and defeated. As an adult, seeing the lives of my friends who seemed to be doing better than me gave me that same feeling. In another old memory, some girls from my class decided to leave me out of their game, and I felt great sadness at being excluded. A few months prior to my unfolding journey, I accidently discovered that one of my friends had hosted a milestone birthday celebration I was not invited to, and I felt deeply hurt when I found out.

The events that caused me pain as an adult looked nearly identical to the events that caused me hurts as a child. And although I had responded to them differently throughout my life, I had not managed to prevent the pain.

A popular quote, widely attributed to the great Albert Einstein, came to mind: "A problem cannot be solved from the consciousness that created it."

Consciousness is a complicated term with all kinds of meanings, but in this context, it refers to the way we view an issue at a fundamental level. The quote implies that this deeper viewpoint determines what we see, and our perceptions then influence our reality. So, if we want to solve a problem, the first step is to dig deeper to shift the underlying beliefs seeding those events.

I once had a teacher explain this idea by using the example of a powerful magnet placed beneath a sheet of paper. Iron filings dropped over the paper will always organize themselves into the same pattern as the shape of the magnet. Changing the sheet of paper or even getting a new set of iron filings will not change the pattern as long as the same magnet lies underneath.

Our core beliefs and perceptions act like that magnet, attracting people and events into our lives. Without changing the magnet of our core beliefs, we will keep experiencing the same events in the same painful cycle.

Over the course of a lifetime or many lifetimes, our perceptions become part of us, ingrained in our biology. These core limiting beliefs are referred to as chakra blockages.

I had read about blockages and how they cause illness and other worldly challenges, but now I was understanding the idea with respect to our emotions. Emotional pain is yet another expression of chakra blockages. Our wounds are no doubt caused by external events, but even those events, like the iron filings in the example, are drawn into our lives on account of our underlying limiting beliefs. A chakra blockage is ultimately a perception that limits the possibilities in the energy center it pertains to, causing repetitive patterns in that area of one's life. Until we uncover and release the perception causing the blockage, true healing cannot happen.

As I looked back at the themes in my own life, I sensed that the intensity of my pain had increased over the years, as if my system was accumulating the feelings over time. I wondered if emotional pain, like physical pain, is nature's way of inviting us to undertake the healing journey. Human beings can be tough and resilient in ways that add to their defenses and not to their deepest well-being. But something bigger than us wants us to wake up and live a more enlightened life. I was sure of that. I needed to find out how to move forward.

***

Even as I explored the chakra system and how I could use it to further understand my own blockages, I continued to drink deep from the wisdom of the *Gita*. In its pages, I found descriptions of a mind that is truly whole and healthy. Such a mind enjoys freedom beyond positivity or negativity and an openness to whatever comes one's way, with neither attachment nor resistance. Fortunately, the *Gita* also lays out a road map for the journey to such wholeness, tracing it through three stages.

The first stage of the journey happens when we are still unaware, blind to the limitations of the world outside or within and cocooned in a false sense of safety and security. Free from fear or any knowledge of our inner child or their wounds, we exist in a complacency born out of either good fortune or denial. Carl Jung referred to this state as "unconscious wholeness."

The second stage begins when something unhappy and unexpected rips open our cocoon of blissful ignorance. Experiencing fear for the first time, we begin to realize that life is not inherently perfect and the world is not always safe. At this stage, we move forward with the goal of pursuing pleasure and avoiding pain, directing our efforts toward controlling our external environment.

The third stage is that of equanimity or wisdom. We arrive at this stage after a great deal of inner work. Finding a deeper identity within, we understand that life's experiences, both happy and sad, do not limit who we truly are. That deeper identity is a common thread that unites us all. By realizing it, we take down the walls that separate us from the world.

I found these three stages fascinating. The more I thought about them, the more I saw the concept of three everywhere. The Christian tradition honors the Trinity of the Father, the Son, and the Holy Ghost. In Hindu mythology, the Hindus represent three energies as the Trinity of Brahma, Vishnu, and Shiva, which are the Creator, Preserver, and Destroyer aspects of God. In Western psychology, Sigmund Freud postulated three major components of human personality: the id, ego, and superego.

In scientific circles, neuroscientist Paul MacLean theorized the triune brain, which suggests that the human brain is organized into three regions that perform three different functions, with the first one being the most primal and the third being the most evolved. MacLean believed that these three parts developed over thousands of years as human beings evolved. Although not all scientists agree with this theory, it is yet another version of the *Gita*'s three mindsets.

Threes also emerge in fairy tales and fables, such as the bears in "Goldilocks and the Three Bears," the three sisters in "Cinderella," and, of course, "The Three Little Pigs." I began to see why we say, "Third time's a charm."

In particular, "The Three Little Pigs" is an apt metaphor for our human journey toward wholeness. In this story, each pig faces the same wolf, but all three respond to the challenge differently. The first two are consumed by the wolf, while the last one succeeds in overcoming the enemy.

Each of us is, indeed, all three little pigs rolled into one, and the wolf that knocks at our door is the recurring issue in our life—the problem that stirs up our inner child's deepest fears and insecurities.

As the first little pig, we start off with a simple and naive approach to life, unaware of any dangers, and we make a house of straw. It is not practical, but it is easy to build—so easy that we are not even aware that we are building a house at all. Then we meet our early disappointments or setbacks from outside us and realize that sometimes life can be unfair and unpredictable. Consumed by fear, we experience the death of the naive first pig after the wolf blows down our house of straw.

The second pig, now burned by disillusionment, believes the wolf lives in the world outside and attempts to keep it at bay. In this stage of our evolution, we armor up through action or avoidance and build our coping mechanisms—our house of sticks—hoping to find lasting safety and well-being. This new house is stronger than the straw house and protects us from danger. But only for a while. Over time, one stick falls, then another, even as we try, again and again, to come up with a permanent solution. Ultimately, the second pig suffers the same fate as the first pig: death in the teeth of the wolf, who blows down our house of sticks.

And then we have the third little pig, who finally outwits the wolf. As the third pig, we build a house of bricks so strong that the wolf cannot blow it down. We choose these bricks with discernment, thanks to the wisdom that lies buried deep within us. And gradually, one brick at a time, we move from seeking change on the outside to finding the key to fearlessness within.

The teachings of the *Gita* were beginning to shed a new light on the human journey for me. When I was a child attending Sunday religion classes in India, there was a great focus on learning the Sanskrit verses of the *Gita* and chanting them as part of our worship. Remembering those days, I wished I had been taught the story of those three pigs instead. It makes me sad to recognize that religious studies too often focus on the letter of the scriptures and miss the spirit.

Closing my reflections for the day, I reminded myself of one of Mother's favorite sayings: "Better late than never." I was thankful to be alive and receiving the teachings now, when I could still apply them to my life.

Tomorrow was another day.

CHAPTER REFLECTIONS

1. What are some recurring patterns in your life that have caused you pain?

2. The first little pig was in ignorance (denial) of the wolf. The second pig tried to avoid it. The third knew that facing the wolf was inevitable and worked hard to be ready when it came around. Where do you see yourself in your journey?

3. What would it take for you to commit to doing the inner work to face reality fearlessly and with equanimity? Is there something that would prevent this?

CHAPTER 6

DISMANTLING THE HOUSE OF STICKS

INSIGHT #4
Success is not a reliable shelter against the "wolf" of shame.

THE STORY OF "The Three Little Pigs," inspired by the three stages described in the *Gita*, was firing up my imagination. The first pig was ignorant, the second was a fixer, and the third was the wise one. I decided to take an honest look at where I stood in my own journey, reviewing my stories through the lens of the three little pigs.

As the youngest child, watching my siblings get into trouble, I quickly outgrew the naivete of the first little pig. Surmising that hard work and perfection were the secret to staying safe, the control-through-hard-work mentality of the second little pig started early and worked for me for many years.

Then, at nineteen, I flunked an important exam in my pursuit of a career as an accountant. I tasted failure for the first time ever. Reeling under its blow,

I struggled for several months with the pain of shame and the loss of control over life that I thought I'd had. At the time, a powerful spiritual teacher had come into my life and initiated me into meditation, thus beginning my spiritual journey. Witnessing the profound changes it brought about in me and my life, I concluded that a spiritual practice had been the missing ingredient in my recipe for a successful life. As I grew into adulthood, more practices followed, along with the number of books and teachings I consumed on spirituality and positivity. Gradually and unconsciously, my practices became a part of the second little pig's tool kit to control events and keep the wolf away.

But now, with my recent string of misfortunes, I was back to the drawing board. All my efforts and practices had not kept my family as happy and cheerful as I had envisioned. Despite my prayers, our son was facing many struggles at his high school, and Mother's cancer had returned. Believing in positivity and resolutely turning away from what was going on was not helping me deal with the harsh realities of my life. Clearly, something was missing.

Picking up the *Gita* to revisit what I saw as the description of the third little pig in its pages, I found just the verses I was looking for:

> He whose mind is untroubled by any misfortune, whose craving for pleasures had disappeared, who is free from greed, fear, anger, who is unattached to all things, who neither grieves nor rejoices if good or if bad things happen—that man is a man of firm wisdom.

Honestly, I was light years away from that ideal. In fact, I was not even walking in that direction! Year after year, I had been working hard for success, not for the wisdom the *Gita* describes. Not that the desire and pursuit of success was wrong in itself. It was the craving that was the problem. Without the freedom that comes from nonattachment, the journey was more about control than true spirituality.

I wanted to get to the bottom of that craving and my relentless need for victory in all the roles I was playing—mother, teacher, and wife, to name a few. Why did I *need* to be successful? What was the wolf that I believed success would save me from? I needed to do more digging to uncover that.

Spending many quiet hours by myself, I resisted the temptation to go back to my to-do lists or call friends and family in an attempt to feel better. Several months had passed since the big dream that had begun my unfolding, and the journaling during this time helped cultivate greater insight when I revisited my stories. While I had started from a place of despair, I was now feeling more curious about my sadness and wanting to understand myself better.

"What do you fear? What do you want?" I asked the girl in red. "Tell me. I am ready to listen."

One morning, an old memory came up that revealed her insecurities more clearly than any memory had before.

It was from a day when I was in kindergarten. The details of the surroundings and the faces of my classmates were hazy, but as the scene unfolded, my emotions were clear.

Our class was preparing for a play in which all the animals and birds of the jungle were plotting together to defeat the big, bad lion. The teacher said she would have us dressed for our roles and that parents would be invited to watch. A big deal in my small world! I rushed home from school all excited.

Grandma, Mother's mother, was visiting us then. She asked me to calm down and tell her what my excitement was all about. Between jumping around and panting for breath, I managed to convey the day's headlines.

"I have a role in the school play!" I announced.

She looked unimpressed. Though not a big woman physically, my grandmother had a big personality and carried a lot of power. For some reason, she loved bursting our bubbles. My brother was spared because he was special.

(Although I did not know it then, in later years, I would learn about her bias toward the male child.)

"They gave you a role, did they? And what would that be?" she asked.

"I am the crow in the jungle!" I sang out in joy.

"The crow? Ha, of course!" she laughed mockingly. "Who else would they give that part to?"

I stopped in my tracks, knowing immediately she was referring to the color of my skin. I was the darkest of her three grandchildren, and she reminded me of it from time to time, calling me by her nickname for me, meaning "Blackie."

I scowled at her, deflated and hurt. *Was I picked for the role only because I look the most like a crow?* I wondered. It had not dawned on me until then that the world saw me as "Blackie" too. I had attributed it only to Grandma.

I said nothing at the time. Children don't talk back to grown-ups. But her unkind words and laughter had returned to me now, years later. Tears belonging to that little girl, unshed from long ago, filled my adult eyes. I sensed what she was revealing to me: her belief and fear that she was basically unlovable.

I drew my inner child close to my heart. Simply acknowledging those little big hurts felt healing.

Being a spiritual teacher all these years, I believed that beauty is skin deep, that words are not sticks or stones, and that the color of the skin is not the color of the soul. But clearly, those messages hadn't reached the child within.

Grandma was not alone in her colorism. As I sat with the memory, similar instances that I had ignored earlier came back to me. Over my school years, I heard many "jokes" about being the darkest child in the class, some even from close friends who did not think it could be hurtful. I had even laughed along, wanting to be a good sport.

From my conversations with her over the years, I knew that Mother had also been a victim of similar ridicule. We were both raised in a culture that favored lighter skin. Whenever I shared such experiences with her, her solution was to pivot from feeling to acting. "Work hard, excel, succeed," she would say. "Show them who you really are!"

Clearly, her attempts to protect me from feeling hurt had led me from being the naive and unaware first little pig into becoming the second one—armoring up with sticks against their stones.

Even as I processed this memory, it was soon followed by one of a different nature. It was very old and took me by complete surprise. It had to do with my name.

My mother had three children, and she wanted our names to be "short and sweet," as she put it. So she named her firstborn, my brother, Ravi, after the God of light, the Sun. Then came my sister, Usha, whose name means "Goddess of the Dawn," in keeping with the theme. Three years later, she had me, an unexpected conception and, as a second girl child, a little unwelcome. While she was preparing for my birth, Mother picked two names, one for a boy and another for a girl. The name she picked for a daughter was "Asha," meaning "Hope."

Traditional Hindus pick a name from the millions of gods and goddesses that the religion offers, believing that the child will enjoy the protection and channel the energies of the chosen deity. The name "Asha" is a human sentiment and does not fall into that category, but Mother liked that it rhymed with my sister's name. Grandma disapproved of the name, but in a rare act of rebellion, Mother named me Asha anyway. So, for the first three or four years of my life, I was Asha to everyone, including myself. Mother and Grandma continued to tussle about this until Mother finally gave in and renamed me Ramaa. Birth certificates in India do not list names, so the change was a simple one to carry out. You just let everyone know the child has a new name, and when they start school, you sign them up using their new name. And that is what my mother did.

All of my life, the only memory I had from that time was a faint recollection of people calling me Asha before the new name settled. But on the morning of this flashback, I was quiet in meditation when a scene unfolded behind my closed eyes. I was about three years old, and Grandma was wagging a finger in front of my scared face and saying, "Asha is bad, very bad! Ramaa is good, very good!"

The memory surfaced, along with a strong visceral reaction. Grandma was a big person to my inner child. Even Mother listened to her! I could feel the huge impact her words had upon the little girl. I leaned into the memory, part of me stepping into that girl's body, wanting to enter the experience from her perspective, while another part, my adult self, watched with compassion, holding space for her. As the girl in red, I felt the pain deeply, now sobbing from the depths of my being. And as the adult witnessing her anguish, I was blown away. The little girl had seen herself as Asha. Hearing that she was "bad," she had taken it personally, believing that she was an ugly secret that needed to disappear under a new name.

I was looking at the scene as if it were a memory from another lifetime, except it wasn't. I had held it in my body for so long. It was as if, beneath my current personality, there was another, hidden self that was feeling illegitimate and trying her best not to be discovered.

As for Grandma, I had a difficult relationship with her all my life. I loved her very much but did not always like her. While she was a great storyteller at bedtime, bought us gifts, and cooked us delicious meals when we visited her every summer, she was also tough and spoke sharp words.

Watching the memory, it was clear that Grandma was simply trying to get me to respond to the new name, and she had done so thoughtlessly. While I wished the grown-ups had taken the time to ease me gently into this change, it was just not how things were done then. Grandma herself had lost her mother when she was still a little girl. Her father had taken a new wife, a young woman who was barely a few years older than his own daughter. Grandma was married off at thirteen and became a mother at sixteen. God alone knew what wounds her inner child carried! As the great teacher and author Louise Hay said, we are "victims of victims."

Grateful that the memory had bubbled up and revealed all this pain, I focused my attention on healing. As the tears flowed, I directed compassion toward my younger self. And when the tears subsided, I reached for my journal, thinking of the right words to shift the energy I was feeling in my body. The first step was to set the record straight with Asha. So I wrote her a letter:

Hello, darling Asha. This is me, Ramaa. Thank you so much for sharing your pain with me. First off, I am sorry that Grandma called you bad. You are not bad. You are Hope, a spark of light, beautiful and flawless in yourself. You belong to me and remain a part of my hopes, my story, and my life. I want to wipe your tears away and hold you close. Please forgive me, and Mom, and Grandma for having hurt your feelings. I will make it up to you, I promise.

After writing the letter, I felt better. Continuing, I wrote the name "Asha" all over my journal page and drew hearts around it. Throughout the rest of my day, I kept up the work, sending kind thoughts and words to that wounded energy in me. It felt like filling the cracks within with love, reminding me of kintsugi, the Japanese art of gluing back broken pieces of pottery with gold.

* * *

I returned to my reflections the next day and honed in on the emotion behind the painful memory. By labeling Asha as bad, Grandma had planted in me the belief that I was intrinsically flawed. This was shame, and the practice of shaming is an old one, passed down from generation to generation as an easy way to get children in line.

"You should be ashamed of yourself!" were oft-repeated words when we were growing up. Another indirect form of shaming came through comparison. Grandma used it all the time, and so did Mother. We were always being compared with children our age—classmates, family friends, and just about anyone who had better grades, behavior, or talents than we did. Usha rebelled against this shaming, often landing in a great deal of trouble, while I worked hard to reach the expected standard.

With the stories that I was uncovering, I now wondered if all my efforts to attain success and hold on to it were just attempts to keep myself safe from facing my basic inadequacy. Was shame the wolf I was running away from? If so, my recent string of failures had shown me that success was not a reliable shelter. It was only a house of sticks, and it was falling apart.

To begin my transformation into the third little pig and build myself a truly sturdy home, I needed to track down the wolf.

CHAPTER REFLECTIONS

1. My house of sticks was success that would keep me from facing my wolf of shame over the labels "Blackie" and "bad." What is your wolf? What is the house of sticks you have built on the outside to defend yourself from it?

2. Look closely at the many roles you play as a spouse, parent, employee, people pleaser, social worker, etc. Which of those roles do you really need to succeed at? Would you love yourself any less if you failed? Why? Your inner child is hidden behind those masks. Find that child and tell them you love them for who they ARE, even when they don't DO so well.

3. Can you remember a story or a conversation that created the wolf of shame in you? Write a letter to your inner child, sending them love, telling them that they belong to you just the way they are, and letting them know that they are beautiful and sacred.

CHAPTER 7

ON THE TRAIL OF THE WOLF

INSIGHT #5
You are not as hurt by what another thinks or says about you as you are by what you believe and how you respond.

IT WAS STILL VERY early in the morning. The rest of my family was asleep, and I was sitting on the couch with my inner-work kit by my side in a plastic box. It held my journal, a little sketchbook, pens, pencils, and crayons. I was in the midst of my morning practice of reflection, journaling, letter-writing, and drawing, now combined with my earlier practices of Yoga, meditation, and breathwork—the latter becoming a significantly smaller part of the hours I had for myself.

My two flashbacks from the week before were still doing their rounds in my mind, and I wanted to see if I could go deeper and tackle shame at its very roots.

So, Grandma called me a crow, I thought. *Why did that hurt so much? Because it was meant to be derogatory with the implication that I was inferior because of my appearance.*

A quote by Eleanor Roosevelt came to mind: "Nobody can make you feel inferior without your consent."

When it comes to shame, like everything else, it takes two to tango. While it was true that Grandma called me Blackie and that friends in school teased me, it was I who believed and internalized that word.

Not that I blamed myself for it. For one thing, I was only a child. For another, there was deep societal conditioning at play.

While we admire birds and animals as they are, our concepts of human beauty are narrow. They are conveyed and reinforced through movies and advertisements, images on posters and billboards, and so on. Even our gods and goddesses are depicted with light skin and tall, slim bodies. No wonder I had bought into the general idea of beauty, whose criteria I did not meet. Although I had been reading and teaching about self-love for years, at the deepest level, there was still a missing piece.

Having descended the staircase and looking now into the eyes of my wounded inner child, it was clear I had allowed the shaming to get to me. It had blown apart my inner sense of security, poisoning my relationship with my inner child, my natural self, the girl in red. Asha. This was the disconnect my dream had revealed.

As a child, I adhered to the rule book not only to please the adults around me but to ensure my own sense of worth, since it was denied from within. This had carried over into adulthood. In addition to my lifelong commitment to self-improvement, I took everything personally and worked hard to compensate for my lapses, whether real or imagined. I knew now that my need to do the right thing was driven by my inner child, who still believed she was not good enough unless she performed well enough.

When we teach our children to ride a bike, we start with training wheels for support and then slowly remove the extra wheels so the children can find their balance from within. But in a culture of comparison and competition, our internal support system becomes debilitated, making us rely upon the external wheels of success and social acceptance for validation.

Shame even infiltrates our relationship with God. The *Gita* speaks of a divine being who sees and loves us for who we are, but the spirit of the message has been lost. Somehow, I had ended up with a God who sought to control us through guilt and punishment. Over the years, I'd had many conversations with friends about Christian guilt, Jewish guilt, and so on. While the spiritual teachings of every faith speak of a Creator who loves us unconditionally, the religious traditions were conveying a conditional love—one that promotes a divide between man and God while creating a schism within oneself.

To make it worse, I had already passed all this on to the next generation. Over the years of parenting my own children, I had also foolishly assumed that shaming is nonviolent and harmless. Believing I was doing the right thing by showing tough love, I had, in reality, been perpetuating the cycle of shame. Not until I connected with my inner child, did I realize shaming's soul-crushing effects.

I had uncovered a multigenerational blind spot of untended self-worth hidden under the strong conviction of being a sincere warrior on life's journey. Shame is self-rejection, and as long as I fed this myth of shame within myself, no amount of validation and success from the world outside could save me. Nor would any spiritual learning or practices.

I added to my reflections: "You are not as hurt by what another thinks or says about you as you are by what you believe and how you respond."

Remembering the words "A problem cannot be solved from the consciousness that created it," I realized that a seismic shift in thinking was needed if my world was going to change.

I concluded my inner work for the day with these words: "Self-acceptance, first. Self-improvement, later. Self-denigration, never."

People-pleasing had always been my first goal. It needed to go. Moving forward, self-acceptance would come first. That meant challenging and changing beliefs I had unconsciously absorbed about identity and self-worth—truths I knew intellectually would now have to be imprinted upon the very fabric of my being so I would feel differently in my body and my emotions.

Releasing Grandma and others from my story, I took responsibility for the pain of my inner child, assuring her that we were in this together and vowing that I would not stop until I had released her pain and replaced it with unconditional love.

CHAPTER REFLECTIONS

1. Despite what Grandma or anyone else said, it was I who was watering the seeds of shame in myself by buying into the beliefs that were handed down to me. Taking responsibility for my inner child's wounds shifted me from being an unconscious victim to an intentional warrior on the journey. Where in your life have you unconsciously assumed the position of a victim? Are you ready to shift from victim to warrior by choosing differently? Are you willing to put in the work it will take to reparent your inner child with new beliefs?

2. Identify one or more beliefs your inner child absorbed that have kept the wounding in place. What would be a new belief that would heal and uplift your inner child? Write the new belief in your journal, and return to it time and again.

CHAPTER 8

ACCEPTANCE— THE FOUNDATION FOR A HOUSE OF BRICKS

INSIGHT #6
There is no escape from adversity.

SELF-ACCEPTANCE. THAT'S WHAT I needed to work on. I began to closely examine the motives behind many of my pursuits. Believing in one's basic inadequacy can spawn a number of people-pleasing actions that may be inauthentic while seeming heartfelt. I even wondered about my meditations and spiritual practices. What parts had been driven by feelings of shame and guilt and a need to please my Creator to earn a happier life?

I had been pondering these thoughts when I came across a quote by spiritual educator and author Elizabeth Lesser:

> Adversity is a natural part of being human. It is the height of arrogance to prescribe a moral code or health regimen or spiritual practice as an amulet to keep things from falling apart. Things do fall apart. It is in their nature to do so. When we try to protect ourselves from the inevitability of change, we are not listening to the soul. We are listening to our fear of life and death, our lack of faith, our smaller ego's will to prevail. To listen to your soul is to stop fighting with life—to stop fighting when things fall apart; when they don't go our way, when we get sick, when we are betrayed or mistreated or misunderstood. To listen to the soul is to slow down, to feel deeply, to see ourselves clearly, to surrender to discomfort and uncertainty and to wait.

I read her words over and over again and reflected on them deeply, as if they came from a sacred text. Adversity is unavoidable. Life happens. Things fall apart. Bad things happen to all people, and not only to the imperfect ones. The idea that difficult times are an inescapable part of the journey was actually freeing. *It was not me after all!* I thought. A visceral relief washed over me.

Suddenly, shame was not the wolf anymore. Adversity was. Shame was, in fact, a defense *against* adversity. By shaming oneself, the ego could hold on to the illusion of complete control. A perfect world was possible if only one changed enough, tried hard enough, or *was* enough.

We were taught to overcome adversity, not to embrace it. Everyone I knew was working hard to keep things from falling apart. Over the years, these attempts had morphed into moral codes resulting in shame and guilt. Even the spiritual practices meant to raise our consciousness had become efforts at appeasing our Creator into giving us an easy life.

I had found my own spirituality at a low point in my life. Over time, I had held on to my spiritual practices like an amulet, something I could do that would prevent another disappointment. My practices had actually *sustained* my fear of adversity. I was beginning to realize the subtle but important difference between practicing a faith tradition and practicing faith itself.

My misconception was a common one. To my surprise, each week, I found myself in conversation with Yoga teachers, healers, and other fellow meditators who, like me, had embraced the spiritual path, believing it was a means to control or escape unpleasant situations. Most of us were educated, high-achieving box-checkers, and our respective practices came from to-do lists designed to get us to our dream lives. And as our stories were unfolding, some were feeling betrayed that life was not as rosy as expected. The more emotional among us were outright denying their reality and trying hard to turn away from the intensity of their feelings, afraid that negativity could bring on more unhappy events. None seemed to have figured out how to relate to the inner world from a place of wisdom.

Although I did not know it then, we were gradually becoming a sangha (short for satsangha), which is a spiritual community rooted in the truth. We were struggling, sharing, and growing together. All of us shared the consciousness of the second little pig, believing and pursuing the myth of a perfect life. But as my own life was revealing, there is no escape from adversity.

Elizabeth Lesser was right. For a human being, hardships are a given.

As for an action plan, her to-do list was mostly a to-be list.

Stay. Surrender. Wait.

None of these came easily to me. I was a fixer. But was my fixing an act of doing? And does waiting actually mean doing nothing?

The *Gita* describes the wise man as "He who can see inaction in the midst of action and action in the midst of inaction."

I was beginning to understand these words. The more we run from our fears, the more we remain stuck in them. And paradoxically, when we stay with our fears—acknowledging and accepting them—we begin moving out of them.

Waiting isn't inaction. Pausing without resisting is an act of courage, a choice to face our demons instead of escaping them. Each time we choose to surrender to the discomfort, we empower ourselves. Embracing adversity means expanding one's mind to make room for loss of control. Releasing old patterns, we prepare to birth a new reality.

I returned to "The Three Little Pigs," when the third little pig builds a house of bricks that the wolf cannot blow away despite his huffing and puffing. Defeated there, the villain then tries to enter through the chimney. But the clever little pig has a fire below. And that is the end of the big, bad wolf.

The third little pig is fully aware that there is no running away from the wolf of adversity, and he is likely to make an appearance again. We need to get ready for this by building a sturdy inner home—baking each nugget of wisdom and cementing it with trust. And as we do that, we stoke the flames of courage, so when the wolf of adversity does knock at the door, our fearlessness can transform misfortune into opportunities for growth.

* * *

I looked at the stories in my journal. Many of them were lost causes I was still holding on to—friendships that had ended badly, opportunities I had missed, guilt over past choices, and so on. Reading them closely, I also got in touch with a more recent, ongoing ache. We had moved to the US planning to return to India after just a few years, but it had been more than ten years since we had arrived. Time had flown by fast, and Krish was enjoying his professional life. Our children saw this country as their home, and relocating to India was practically out of the question at this stage. Yet I had not come to accept it and was nurturing a homesickness that passively resisted the status quo of our reality. While the rest of the family had embraced American citizenship, I had firmly held on to my Indian passport and to my longing to be part of the family events and celebrations happening on the other side of the planet.

Time had moved on, and it was only I who had been keeping these issues alive. Since Mother had inspired us to never give up, I had become an expert in holding on. But holding on is not victory. Nor is acceptance defeat. On the contrary, true acceptance is a choice that ends victimhood.

I was ready to let go of resistance to unchangeable things and trust life as it was, in that moment. But I simply did not have the muscle for letting go. It needed to be built, like an asana in Yoga that is mastered through practice.

My journal had already become much more than a depository for my feelings. It had become my Yoga mat, the place where I would work on weightlessness training, unburdening myself from the heaviness of the past, and move forward gracefully.

I wrote in my journal: "Acceptance is a choice, a gift, a pathway to freedom and empowerment."

And then I began listing the events and outcomes of the past that could not be changed. When I was done, I put my journal aside, closed my eyes, and took a deep breath, preparing to do a visualization exercise.

In my imagination, the little girl in red held a bunch of balloons. On each balloon was a word that represented a lost cause on the outside or a dark label that she had internalized and needed to release. There were so many that she struggled to remain steady on her feet. My adult self knelt by her side and said gently, "You can let those go now."

Their strings were tangled around her little fingers, some more closely than others. I imagined detangling them slowly and intentionally, beginning with the oldest ones. "Blackie" was one, "Bad Asha" another. Then there was one with the name of a friend I had lost a long time ago. Together, we released the balloons and watched as they floated away, one by one. I exhaled as each one left my body's filing cabinet.

But there were some still left. My inner child was reluctant to set them all free at once, so I let her keep the remaining. We would release them another time. Feeling much lighter after my visualization, I knew the next day would bring forth new challenges, of course, but the exercise had lifted my spirits, and I promised myself that I would continue the visualization exercise for a few weeks more.

In the days that followed, I reached out to our family's immigration attorney and filed my application for American citizenship. I was finally taking my first step toward accepting my reality.

CHAPTER REFLECTIONS

1. I had been taught to overcome adversity, not to make room for it. What about you? Did Elizabeth Lesser's words on adversity strike a chord with you? Read the quote again, and reflect on the wisdom of accepting what cannot be changed.

2. To let go of past regrets, lost causes, and disappointments and to make room in your life for something new, try the following exercise. Visualize a bunch of balloons with long strings, each one having a word or words that represent something you would like to let go of. What are the words you picked? Now let go of the balloons. For the ones that get tangled up, try to remove just one knot every day and see if you can sense the relief, however small it might be.

CHAPTER 9

GUILTY UNTIL PROVEN RESPONSIBLE

INSIGHT #7
Guilt is neither spiritual nor holy.

ONE DAY, WHILE WAITING for my friend Sharon to get ready for our walk together, I sat in her living room, watching football with her husband, Bob. During a pause in the action, the players circled together on the field.

"What's going on?" I asked Bob hesitantly. "Is something wrong?"

"No, that's just a huddle," he replied shortly, returning his attention to the screen.

I had no idea what that meant and wanted to know more. Rather than interrupt Bob again, I looked it up when I returned home and found the description on Wikipedia: "In sport, a huddle is an action of a team gathering together, usually in a tight circle, to strategize, motivate, or celebrate. Commonly the leader of the huddle is the team captain and it is the captain who will try to inspire other team members to achieve success."

I knew immediately why the concept appealed to me. There were many contrasting voices within myself, and a huddle was a great way to get them to work together toward the goal of healing. There was my internal cheerleader and my inner critic, my deep emotional self and my rational thinker, the fixer and the scaredy cat, among several others.

A morning huddle soon became part of my daily routine. It was a time for checking in, listening, planning, and making decisions so I could move forward with my day intentionally.

I held this internal huddle in my heart center, the meeting ground for the opposites within me. As the leader of Team Ramaa, I would begin by inviting all the thoughts and emotions that showed up that day. Some days, many voices showed up, and on other days, there were only a few. After taking a few slow breaths for everyone in the huddle to calm down, I would review the agenda for the day—the places I had to be and the meetings on my calendar. Setting my intentions for each appointment, I would get all or at least most of the members of my personal team to align with it. If an issue was bothering me, it would be taken up at the huddle, and I would look at it from many angles, attempting to arrive at the best possible response. Even during the day, if I received disturbing news or an unpleasant email, I would quickly and briefly retire to a quiet place, call for a quick huddle, and spend a few minutes regrouping. Often, just acknowledging the various voices and breathing together helped me move forward.

Over time, I was gradually cultivating the discernment to recognize the role of various voices in my head and deal with them more intentionally. Not surprisingly, a couple of loud members of the team were guilt and shame. When something went wrong, they would be the first voices I would hear. Thanks to my upbringing, for years, I had chosen to support them as good, and even necessary. But now I was reviewing their role in weakening the team spirit. Guilt had some healthy components, no doubt, bringing about accountability. But more often, it was unhealthy perfectionism, or "the ego's will to prevail," as Elizabeth Lesser had pointed out. As for shame, it was sheer rebellion against who nature created me to be.

With my daily huddle, I was able to bring down the voices of guilt and shame while amplifying the voice of self-appreciation, which had been barely a whisper.

As the months passed, I longed to share my insights with Mother. The opportunity for that came sooner than I expected, and it was a conversation that would've been impossible without my huddle.

* * *

It was a Thursday afternoon. I was just wrapping up class with a close group of women when my cell phone rang. I was surprised that I had left the volume on since I usually turned it off before beginning a session. I reached to silence it but saw that it was Usha. It was the early hours of morning in India. I knew what the call meant, and it was not good.

Dad's stroke had led to dementia, and it had gotten worse in the past year. Meanwhile, Mother's cancer was relentless. She was still working at her high-powered job as administrator of a leading eye hospital, a role she loved. Between her work and her failing health, it had been very difficult for her to care for our father. Earlier in the year, Usha and her wonderful husband had moved Dad into their home. Despite her own challenges, Mother had protested at first, wanting to soldier on, but we had finally convinced her.

An engineer by profession, Dad had worked in an automobile factory, mostly on the late-night shift. When we were growing up, he left for work when we were in school and returned home when we were asleep. We were quiet as we prepared to go to school so as not to disturb him while he slept. His weekly day off was Friday, while we were home from school only on Sundays, so we saw little of him on weekends as well. Mother was the principal parent; it was only after he retired that we spent any time with Dad. Still, there was deep affection in the relationship, and we knew he had worked hard for our family despite hardly enjoying himself. Although Mother remained our go-to parent for day-to-day struggles, we had each become closer to Dad in recent years, and it was painful to witness his decline.

When I called a few days earlier, Usha gave Dad the phone. But there was no conversation, and my heart wept silent tears as he merely said my name nonstop until she gently took the phone back. He was sinking. I knew that, but I had not expected this call so soon.

My Thursday afternoon group was a small one, and we had been learning and growing together for many years now. I was most comfortable with this group and took the call without hesitation.

"It's over," Usha said. "He's gone."

"Were you with him?" I asked.

"Oh yes, I held his head in my lap as he passed."

"Bless you," I whispered as I heaved a sigh of farewell. After a few more questions, I hung up the phone and returned to my group.

I did not know what to feel. It was my first time losing a parent. The women hugged me close and stayed with me while I gathered my thoughts. I needed to leave for India soon.

I took a couple of weeks off so Mother and I could spend a good deal of time together between visitors' condolences and the death rituals for Dad's passing.

* * *

Mother had lost more weight since the last time I had seen her, and it felt strange to be with her. I couldn't imagine her as a widow, and, as it turned out, she couldn't either. She had married my father at the age of eighteen, and it had been a marriage full of challenges. Yet she had wanted to be the first one to go. In the Hindu tradition, a woman who dies before her husband enjoys special privileges in the afterlife. A common blessing for a married woman is "May you die before your husband" or "May you never experience widowhood."

Dad's passing had left her in a rare state of vulnerability, and she was willing to talk about difficult emotions. Having been raised to believe widowhood was a demotion, she shared with me how deeply it affected her that Dad went first. I sensed more shame than grief and used the opportunity to share some of my thoughts on the subject.

I said to her, "These are absurd patriarchal myths, Mother. A woman is not any less without her man. Your identity is primarily yours. You are a strong woman and have always been, widow or not."

My words brought her some relief, but I could see something still bothered her. She revealed it the next afternoon as we slowly sipped our chai together.

"There is one thing I cannot get over," she began.

"What is that?" I asked.

"I feel so guilty that I was not there by Dad's side when he passed. I should have never let you and Usha talk me into moving him to her place. It was my dharma to take care of him. I am not sure God will ever forgive me for this."

Mom's body was frail, but her will was as strong as ever. She had not neglected Dad at all. She had made arrangements for his care and visited him regularly during the previous nine months, right up to the night he passed away. He had breathed his last a few hours after she had left Usha's place. Her guilt made no sense, but I understood it only too well.

It had been three years since my first dream, and I was still working through a lot of memories of guilt and shame myself. Having deep conversations about feelings was not Mother's thing, but Dad's passing had given me the opening I was waiting for. I decided it was time to share some of my views and insights with her during her own difficult time.

"Mother, I'm not sure God has anything to do with what you're feeling," I began. "He left it to us to decide our dharma, and we must each face the results of our choices."

"Oh no!" Her dissent was quick and filled with conviction. "God gave us our dharma and asked us to abide by it. He tells us what our duty is, and we do it. Mine was to look after your dad through thick and thin, and I failed at it."

The subject of duty and who gets to define it was close to both my head and my heart. I knew it well.

"That is not how I understand God's word," I persisted, getting up for my copy of the *Gita*, which I always traveled with.

I said, "Dharma or duty was not meant to be a common regimen to be blindly followed by everyone, Mother. It's a personal choice based on our individual nature. Each of us needs to own our unique strengths and inclinations and play the part our soul has decided upon. Listen to these words: 'Know your Dharma and do it without hesitation.' And this verse too: 'Better to do your own dharma badly than to do another's perfectly.'"

I went on. "You have lived an authentic life. You are an amazing leader. Your organizational and people skills have helped everyone at the hospital where you work. Your colleagues have nothing but praise and gratitude for your long service. You've done your dharma, Mother."

"Oh, at the hospital, sure," she said. She seemed to dismiss her years of hard work as she continued. "But I should have stayed home and taken care of your dad. I wish I had listened to my conscience on this."

She, like so many others, had mistaken cultural conditioning as the voice of her own conscience.

"Conscience or cultural guilt, Mother?" I asked.

She looked at me, not understanding.

I decided to lay it all out. Taking a deep breath, I went on.

"That is not your conscience speaking. That is the voice of your upbringing that shames you for being different from most women your age. When Usha and I were kids, you were the only one among my friends' mothers who worked. As you aged, when your friends were looking forward to quietly babysitting their grandchildren, you aspired to freedom from traditional roles. You grew from strength to strength. Now, in your seventies, you are the only one of your contemporaries still holding a job and doing so well at it."

"Yes, but look at what happened." Mother continued with her guilty refrain. "I was not there when Dad passed. I think it is God punishing me for failing in my duty. I should have done better."

Despite all her professional achievements, she had clearly internalized society's judgment for being her own person. Now she imagined it to be God's wrath upon her.

"Mother, that is just the ego speaking because you were not by Dad's side when he passed away. Maybe that was how it was always meant to end. Dad died content, in Usha's lap. I cannot think of a better way to go."

"Then why do I feel so guilty?" she lamented.

I was grateful for the inner work I had done in recent years that helped me recognize her pain. I spoke slowly. "Because, Mother, self-flagellation with shame and guilt is the only way you were taught to deal with disappointments." I paused, adding, "In fact, you handed that down to me as well."

Mom suddenly sat up. "What do you mean?"

She always said being our mother was a job she had taken very seriously. Knowing how she would react to my words, I was nervous, even wanting to drop the conversation. But an internal cacophony from my huddle pushed me forward. The voices of my inner missionary and cheerleader were egging me on. Even my inner critic was on board, asking me not to shut down now that I was here. When my inner philosopher pointed out that speaking my truth was my dharma, I decided to continue.

"Well, whenever I was in any difficult situation, your first question to me was always, 'And what was your role in all of this?' Whether it was me complaining about some kid in school or someone accusing me of something, my own guilt was a foregone conclusion. I was always the one doing the apologizing. I was never entitled to an apology myself."

Mother listened and was quiet for a long moment. And then she said slowly, "If I were to raise you all over again, I would still do just that."

What? I thought. Then, in disbelief, I asked, "Why?"

"Because," she explained, "that's how you raise children to grow them into responsible adults. There are rights and wrongs in this world. Guilt ensures that you take responsibility for your choices and their consequences. I was never one to spoil my children with blind affection. Would any of you be who you are without such an upbringing?"

I took that in. As difficult as it was to receive, I was beginning to see where she was coming from. I could also see the point she was missing.

"Mother, I agree. There are right choices and wrong choices. And you have taught us to make the right ones. But even when we make decisions that feel right at the time, they can have unexpected, disappointing outcomes. There are no guarantees. When you raise a child with guilt, they are seeking control, which we don't have. I have struggled for years. When I see the challenges my children are facing from living in a culture and a world that is so different from our home, I have felt like a failure for causing that. These past years, when I have heard that Usha is taking you or Dad for your doctor appointments and I am unable to be of use to anyone, I have felt guilty for choosing to live abroad. Guilt has been my prison for so long. It is only through reading the *Gita* that I have come to accept that every decision we make has unintended consequences and that we need to accept it and play our part anyway. Listen to this."

I read aloud again. "'No one should relinquish his duty, even though it is flawed; all actions are enveloped by flaws, as fire is enveloped by smoke.'" Then I said, "See? The *Gita* accepts that a perfect choice is impossible. Our dharma is only to make the best choice in our given circumstances. We must face whatever it brings. Moving Dad to Usha's place was the right decision, given your work and your own health. So stop beating yourself up as if it could change the past."

"I know I cannot change the past," Mom said, looking tired and defeated. "But if I did make a mistake, God will know I am suffering from guilt and will forgive me."

She made it sound like guilt was an insurance premium one paid to obtain the coverage of grace if and when one faced the Creator. *Is this relationship with the divine coming from faith or fear?* I wondered.

I tried again. "Feeling guilty is not the same as taking responsibility. God does not want you to carry that burden, Mother. Just the opposite, in fact. Here, let me read you something else."

I quickly picked up the *Gita* again and read one of my favorite verses: "'Relinquishing all dharmas, take refuge in me alone. Do not fear. I will free you from the evils of birth and death.' See that assurance? The Christians say, 'Let go, Let God.' It is the same message everywhere. All religions have their rituals for repentance, after which you move on. There is nothing holy about guilt. Think about this—even a terrible criminal is imprisoned for a time and then set free. But not so with guilt. It is the ego's prison, one that never sets us free. We have to claim that freedom by taking refuge in a forgiving God."

Mother sat silent for several moments, pensive and wrapping her mind around this. Then her expression slowly softened. The sun of self-acceptance was beginning to break through the dark clouds of her guilt. She wept quietly, and I held her close. I was crying too. Not only for the loss of my earthly father but also for the loss of a heavenly Father whom neither of us had been raised with. A God who loved us for ourselves and supported our efforts on Earth—not a perfectionistic, punishing God. I lamented being separated from the God of the *Gita*, written five thousand years ago, through an interpretation that had completely missed the truth: We are loved. We are held. Unconditionally.

* * *

The rest of my stay unfolded peacefully. Mom soon recovered from that rare meltdown. When she spoke to visitors who came to offer condolences later that evening, I heard her voice return to its usual confidence. While a part of me was glad, I also missed the emotional connection we had shared during that precious window of vulnerability.

I ruminated on our conversation for a few days, and in the little guest bedroom of the apartment where she and Dad had lived, I journaled about our exchange. As I reflected on Mother's guilt, an old memory came back to me—the story of Mother's birth that Grandma had long ago told me, which revealed the deep roots of her warrior spirit. When Grandma was in the throes of labor, her father, an astrologer, prepared the chart of the child in the birth canal. As he noted the positions of the various planets, he was excited and thrilled. It was an excellent chart for a male child, with all the traits that would help him thrive. Upon learning that his newborn grandchild was a female, my great-grandfather's face fell in dismay. He later said to my grandmother, "Your daughter will face many odds. As a great male energy in a woman's body, life will challenge her at every step."

Remembering that story now, I understood Mother's life differently and the struggles she faced in being her authentic self. Her life had not been an easy one. She did indeed have many challenges to overcome. Some were simply life's misfortunes, and some were because of her own nature, just as her grandfather had predicted.

In her time, even more so than now, culture shamed a woman for feeling the masculine emotions of ambition and enterprise; likewise, men were shamed for being unambitious and diffident. Although she did all she could in her various roles, there was the unbridgeable chasm in her inner world between who she was and who she secretly believed she should be. Fearless in the world outside, what scared Mother most was her own natural self.

Guilt filled this gap, and she held on to it with a sincere belief that she was compensating for her innate inadequacy. As a parent, she had applied this same principle, using the tools of guilt and shame as cookie cutters over each of her children's natural dispositions.

I felt a deep compassion for Mother in a way I had never felt before. Her cancer was of the digestive organs—perhaps because of her struggle to digest her own unpalatable nature owing to the enculturated shame of being a powerful woman. Courage without serenity can bring down a system.

***

Flights heading west from India take off at ungodly hours to accommodate the needs of people at the destination. Mother had accompanied me to the airport, a tradition she kept up faithfully until her cancer completely took over. As I settled into my seat for the long flight home, I imagined her returning to her empty home and new reality, and I wiped a tear. First thing in the morning, she would clear up the few things of Dad's that remained at the apartment and then throw herself back into work.

Recalling our earlier conversation, I remembered her words about wanting us to be responsible adults. I was responsible all right, but a lot of my hard work had come from a place of guilt, compensating for the innate imperfection of my inner child. What would responsibility feel like when it came from a healthy place of intention and enthusiasm? How would it look when it was an expression of inspiration, not inadequacy? It seemed like a long way to get there.

I closed my eyes and tried to catch some sleep.

CHAPTER REFLECTIONS

1. An internal huddle represents various aspects of ourselves—our lofty goals and ideals, as well as our earthly desires and fears. Often, there are many voices to hear. As the head coach, confer with your team every morning to review the past and plan the future. Imagine your team breathing together as one and putting forth the intentions for the day. At the end, take a deep breath, and start the day over with the words "Go team!"

2. Reflect on your relationship with guilt. When and how often do you act out of guilt and fear?

3. Do you believe carrying guilt will please God and release you from your wrongdoing?

4. Write two letters. The first to God or the Universe, asking to be forgiven for your wrongdoings. For the second letter, imagine yourself as an unconditionally loving God, then write yourself a response to your first letter, unburdening you from the weight of guilt and setting you free. Read this second letter every day, and release the past.

5. What would it take for you to move forward and make choices out of love and accountability toward yourself instead of acting from guilt? What would that look like?

PART 3

LESSONS AND LEARNING

CHAPTER 10

TEACHINGS FOR A NEW CONSCIOUSNESS

INSIGHT #8

Mother Nature masterminds our transformation.

RETURNING TO THE US, I resumed my usual routine, including my weekly calls to Mother. She had already been living alone for several months, since Dad had moved to Usha's house, so it was easy to pick up where we had left off. Mother returned to her strong, positive self and did not bring up our deep exchange again. We were back to the same old conversations and updates. I longed for more but soon accepted the status quo and moved on with doing my own inner work and teaching my classes.

One morning, a few months later, I had just finished leading a session and was gathering my notes when Audrey, one of the ladies in my group, approached me with a book in her hand. It looked very thick and reminded me of the textbooks I had read as a student.

"Hi, Audrey. What is that book?" I asked as she sat on the floor in front of me.

"It's a gift for you," she said with her sunny smile. "I came across it in the store, and it had your name written all over it."

It was Anodea Judith's *Eastern Body, Western Mind: Psychology and the Chakra System as a Path to the Self*. I couldn't believe my eyes! There was a book on the exact subject that had consumed my interest these past years! It had not even occurred to me to look for one. I thanked Audrey and all those invisible hands that had brought this book into mine.

I began reading that same night. Audrey was right. This book was just what I needed. Anodea's work focuses on the strong human experiences of shame, fear, loss, and so on, framing them within the chakra system. Her words confirmed my own recent insights. In addition, Anodea brings in perspectives from Western psychology, which further deepened my understanding of emotions.

I devoured the book, filling the margins with notes to myself and highlighting thousands of quotes. At every step, Anodea's work integrates our desires for earthly success with our deeper yearnings for spiritual growth, and I loved it. For years, my healing efforts had been centered around success as the way to feel secure and worthy. Now, with my house of sticks dismantled, I was learning that success without inner growth is as unsteady as a mirage.

One quote in particular stood out to me: "We either get success or lessons. If we learn our lessons successfully, we get both."

Only by internalizing the lessons can we build a safe haven in and for ourselves.

When I finished reading her book, I reached out to Anodea to thank her for writing such a comprehensive work. She replied promptly, inviting me to join a weeklong workshop she was leading based on the book. I was delighted and went to California to join twenty or so other women to do some deep digging and healing.

On the first day, Anodea set out the week's plan. Every morning would begin with a Yoga practice centered around a certain chakra. The rest of the day would be dedicated to teachings and discussions related to that chakra. Anodea asked us to partner with a fellow participant who would serve as our guardian angel for the week. Each evening, we would be assigned topics for reflection with our guardian angels. My guardian angel was a lovely woman, Gail, from California. She was intuitive, insightful, funny, and kind. From the get-go, we were drawn to one another and quickly became soul sisters.

The week went by fast. Taking in Anodea's teaching, I saw our energy centers as inexhaustible fields of knowledge. She stressed the importance of embodying a new consciousness, beyond intellectual acceptance or understanding.

"What you cannot hold, you cannot have," she would say, meaning that unless our entire body, mind, and choices were in alignment with our spirit, we would not be able to sustain our successes in the material world. The Yoga and breathwork enabled the release of our old, limiting messages encoded within the physiology of each chakra, and I experienced healing at a new level.

On the last evening, Gail and I sat down for our final soul talk. We were close to the dormitory, sitting on a comfortable bench beneath a large tree. The evening was cold, and we both huddled in blankets we had brought over from our rooms. I had been feeling overwhelmed with struggles in nearly all areas of my life and was pouring my heart out. Gail listened with compassion while sharing some of her own challenges. We sat there till late in the evening, until the sun went down. As it got colder, we headed indoors.

Dragging my heavy blanket behind me, I was leading the way up the stairs to our rooms when I heard Gail give a small shout.

"Wow, look at these!"

I turned around to see her pointing to my blanket. Looking down then, I saw them too. Caterpillars—several of them—crawling across the fabric. Gail began counting them. There were seven in all. To my untrained eye, they were just caterpillars. But being more intuitive, Gail saw this as no coincidence.

With great excitement, she declared, "This is a message for you from nature! We were sitting under the same tree, but there are none on my blanket. Look!" She held it up for me and then went on. "Caterpillars are symbols of transformation. And there are seven of them, one for each chakra. Ramaa, you are on a journey of growing into a butterfly. I am so happy for you!"

I looked disbelievingly, both at the caterpillars crawling on my blanket and at Gail's clean one. It was weird indeed, and I was still unsure what to make of it. But the next morning, Anodea confirmed Gail's interpretation.

"A great deal of growth happens to us when we seem stuck in situations we cannot run away from," she said, encouraging me to stay the course of whatever I was facing.

I reflected on this sign, knowing the transformation from caterpillar to butterfly, from stuck in place to taking flight, is more than a change in form. It is a paradigm shift, a total reconstruction of one's reality from the inside out.

I once heard someone say that a work in progress often looks like a mess. The caterpillars had been sent to tell me that my prolonged dejection was a work in progress. And to remind me that all transformational journeys are orchestrated by Mother Nature.

Despite my gloomy mood, I felt a flicker of hope. The idea of a bigger vision held a promise of light at the end of the tunnel.

* * *

Many teachers and their teachings continued to come my way after that. It felt like raw material was landing in my lap every day. Wisdom for me to reflect on and apply to my life came like the many bricks I needed to build a stronger house within.

At my physical home, my struggles continued. Our daughter was now a preteen with a keen sensitivity to messages from the environment. We were raising our children in a predominantly Caucasian neighborhood, and once again, in an entirely different place and time, I was becoming aware of how the color of one's skin affects one's perceptions, emotions, and experiences. In the years since my big dream, I had realized that self-approval was an inside job and was working on it myself. Now I had my children joining me on the journey.

My one consolation was that I was not alone in my struggles. Through several conversations with other mothers in my sangha, I understood that we all suffered from the same insecurities, although our stories were different. Our ancestors had lived through wars, economic depressions, and other hardships and had mostly focused on survival. Success and assimilation into the culture had been considered far more important than inner lives. None of us had been taught how to accept and transform our suffering into growth.

But times were changing, and our emotions, which had been suppressed within us for many years, had returned with a sudden, demanding intensity. This emergence of generational emotional awareness seemed to be a worldwide phenomenon, with many calling it the return of the divine feminine.

The world at large, as well as my small one, was finally waking up to the truth that one size does not fit all. We are all human, and we are all different. The return of the divine feminine requires us to each make room for our uniqueness and integrate it into our day-to-day lives and relationships.

I just didn't know yet *how* to do that within my family.

* * *

I had continued to meet with Jackie, my dream interpreter, from time to time as we worked through other less significant dreams. She would often speak about the divine feminine and refer to Carl Jung as a pioneer in that work. I did not know much about him. The only Western name I associated with psychology had been Sigmund Freud. Yet Jackie's tutorials always fascinated me.

One day, quite unexpectedly, I was researching something online and was delighted to learn that Carl Jung had written a commentary about Kundalini Yoga and the symbolism of the chakras. Intrigued, I bought the book and dove into Jung's analysis of the chakra system as a way to access our hidden filing cabinets, which he referred to as the unconscious.

Not long after, I came across a two-year program on Jungian psychology offered by the C. G. Jung Institute of Chicago. I wanted to enroll in the program right away but learned that it required the applicant to be a psychotherapist, which I was not. I felt greatly disappointed and tried to let it go.

My huddle was still part of my daily practice. I used it to check in, share ups and downs, ask for support, or offer it to any of my selves that needed it. I shared my disappointment that I could not be admitted into a program that sounded like just what I needed. We put that into our wish list during the closing meditation.

The very next day, I received another email about the program. They had relaxed the requirement, inviting non-therapists who were in the field of spiritual counseling to apply! I felt a magical hand at work and made my application.

I knew almost nothing about Jung when I started the program, and I was grateful for that. It left me open to receiving each new piece of information with amazement.

Carl Jung, like the ancient *Gita*, written long before his work, rooted his teachings in human nature. While conventional psychotherapy focused on nurture and early childhood, Jung's approach integrated nurture with nature, along with one's connectedness to the collective. Carl Jung became known as the "midlife therapist," and his methods were geared toward aligning a person with their original self.

Jung had studied religions and their impact on the human psyche, and a good part of the course discussed rituals across various traditions. I had a new appreciation for some of the rituals I had been raised with and recommitted to them with even more respect.

Early in the program, we learned about the Myers-Briggs Personality Test (MBTI), conceptualized by Carl Jung. Although we are all born equal, we are configured differently, and this test laid out the four principal areas in which our differences lie: where we focus our attention, how we take in information, how we arrive at decisions, and how we deal with the world. Based on these four differentiators, Jung's students created the Myers-Briggs Personality Test, which lays out sixteen types of individuals.

Studying the MBTI brought me back to my reflections on the caste system in India. I saw parallels to the *Gita*. Both approaches—one a recent test, and the other an ancient text—had four basic differentiators, and both were attempting to identify and organize inherent human differences. Studying the MBTI reinforced my interpretation that the caste system of the *Gita* is not intended to delineate a social class structure but rather to empower individuals to live life based on their natural proclivities.

I also deeply appreciated Jung's two frameworks for decision-making: thinking versus feeling. Thinkers rely more on their thoughts and facts, while feelers lean more into their sentiments and feelings.

Nature had not created a right and a wrong way to choose. It is just that we live in a world where the divine masculine rules, and thinking has been prioritized and deified over feeling. In this off-balance world, emotions are considered both unreliable and weak. Strength is measured in terms of one's ability to repress emotions and follow their rational side. But in the new language I was learning through the MBTI, both thinking and feeling are simply human functions, and they refer to working with both from an awareness that does not place one above the other.

This view felt freeing. I heaved a gentle sigh of relief as though I had been holding my breath from a very, very long time ago, waiting for a signal that it was okay to feel so deeply.

Another piece of wisdom came through learning about extraversion versus introversion, a key differentiator in the MBTI. I was surprised to learn that these qualities have nothing to do with one's social skills. Instead, they're determined by where we find clarity and renewal. Extraverts find their energy primarily through interaction with others, while introverts find it within. This explanation again answered so many questions for me.

Fascinated, I listened to the presentation of these types. There were twenty-three of us in the program, and I was the only one with no background in psychotherapy. Still, when I looked around, I could see that my classmates were just as absorbed. I returned to my thoughts, which were clicking into place so rapidly that I could feel my heart beating faster. Based on what I was learning, Mother's type was different from mine, quite the opposite in each of the four areas. My son, interestingly enough, was closer to his grandmother than to me. The challenges in communication that I was facing in these relationships suddenly began to make so much sense.

When I signed up for the program, I had no idea what I would find, but here already was a big treasure. I was understanding the differences within my family without judgment for the first time, and it felt, finally, like I could address these consciously, although I still had no control over them.

* * *

Once home from the weekend's presentation, I made my family take the test. We discussed our individual traits and blind spots openly. Going online, we found the MBTI types of celebrities and shared many aha moments and laughs together. Typology had made it safe for us to show up as ourselves and brought about a new awareness and respect for our differences. As we played a board game after dinner, I looked at the beloved faces of my family and felt a surge of joy. I was finally learning to see them as they were instead of through my own needs and expectations.

After so many years of trying to fit into who I thought I should be, I was on a path toward accepting and appreciating the uniqueness of my inner child—the person I was born to be. And it was flowing into all my relationships. I was finally realizing that we cannot truly love another unless we see and accept them for who they are, and we cannot do that without seeing and accepting ourselves first.

I shared my insights with the groups I was teaching. Already my lessons, which had started with meditation and Kundalini Yoga, had morphed into psychospiritual discussions and book study groups focused on conscious living. Making room for our intrinsic differences meant that our ways of working, parenting, and pretty much everything else would need to weave in those differences.

Maya Angelou said, "When you know better, you do better." But knowing better did not automatically translate into doing better. It needed intentional effort to build new responses.

In the coming months, encouraged by Anish, my son, I trained for a certification to administer the MBTI test. It became part of my tool kit. When helping couples or families, I often had them take the test so they could understand their issues at a deeper level. Together, we worked to find solutions that integrated their differences. This felt closer to living a life of dharma, or responsibility, in the way the *Gita* speaks about rather than trying to fit people into predetermined frameworks.

I thought about the staircase in my big dream. How is it that every culture, religion, and test tries to force our unique differences into a hierarchy, with some at the top and some at the bottom? I could no longer ascribe to this vertical order. My internal value system was undergoing profound changes, and I felt myself bridging the gap with each step down that staircase.

Slowly, but surely.

CHAPTER REFLECTIONS

1. Could any part of your ongoing sadness or anger be nature attempting to bring about a deeper transformation in you? Can you see the work in progress in the midst of the mess?

2. Are you familiar with the MBTI or any other test that helps you get in touch with your natural traits and tendencies? Has it helped you better understand yourself, your emotions, and your reactions? If you are not familiar with it, consider taking the MBTI here: https://www.mbtionline.com/en-US/Products/For-you/

3. Reflect on the idea that you were created by Mother Nature to be just who you are, as is everyone else in your life. Make peace with the differences between you and your world of family, friends, and associates.

CHAPTER 11

ON MY OWN

INSIGHT #9

Identifying with our inherent traits limits and divides us.

A S I DEEPENED MY study of the Myers-Briggs Personality Test, I began addressing old dilemmas. The far-reaching impact of one type of parent raising a child of a completely different type was dawning upon me.

Everything in nature needs to be nurtured in a certain way in order to thrive. When you buy plants, they come with instructions. Some thrive in the sun, and some in the shade. A plant that needs sunlight but is deprived of it will not grow into its full potential, just as a plant that needs shade withers in bright sunlight. Children, however, do not enter the world with instructions. Cultural and parental biases influence the way we are raised, leaving us with unintended baggage that we barely even see or understand.

I thought of my extended family and friends, trying to guess each person's MBTI type and wondering how their lives may have been impacted by unconscious parenting or partnerships. By seeing people with this new lens of their inner mental-emotional framework, I experienced a new and deeper appreciation of their struggles and successes.

All of these reflections changed the way I taught my classes. I began to see the need for adults to re-parent themselves to nurture their natural selves into healthier adulthoods.

I was moving further away from the conventional practices of breathwork and chanting. More and more, I employed the various tools of self-reflection as a pathway to healing the blockages in the chakras. I administered the MBTI test during my classes or assigned it as homework and invited students to interpret their struggles in light of their findings.

In my own inner work, I revisited several memories from my childhood from this perspective. Jung's thinking versus feeling function had particular relevance for me. Over the years and even now, Mother would encourage me to stop focusing on my emotions when I was upset and instead undertake some "useful" project. She would come up with suggestions for what I could do to cheer myself up. Clearly, she leaned more toward being a thinker, and I was more of a feeler. While her thinking function had carried our family through many crises in the past, it blocked her understanding of my emotional struggles.

Over the years, I had faithfully followed Mother's guidance, believing in her more than I believed in my own feelings. But I could no longer do so. Thanks to the climate at home with two sensitive youngsters and my own heightened midlife sensitivity, these days, I was reacting even more emotionally to everything.

One morning, feeling heartbroken over a falling-out with a dear friend in the neighborhood, I called Mother. I was hoping for some comforting words, but she seemed uninterested in even listening to the details. Her cut-to-the-chase words of advice brought on a sense of déjà vu: "Stop feeling so bad. Just apologize and move on!"

With my recent study of the MBTI, I realized how much easier it had always been for her to do just that. For my own emotional nature, there had to be another way. I stepped away from that conversation without the old sense of being a failure. I was also beginning to understand what had transpired between us all along.

I had always idolized Mother. She handled everything in our family with her confident, extraverted, thinker style. She was my heroine and role model. I looked a lot like her, too, so when people commented on our resemblance, I puffed up with a quiet pride. My one aim in life was to be like her, and rarely, if ever, did I have a view of my own.

Mother often sneered at "quiet, emotional types," referring to them as weak. And although I followed her lead and adopted her opinions to be like her, my own reactions to everything had always been emotional. Overriding my real and weaker self to be who I thought I should be, I often felt like a sham. Now, I realized that my emotions were not a weakness but part of my database, a principal source of information. The intensity of my emotions after all these years was Mother Nature asserting herself. She had made me like this, and the wise path forward was to accept my internal programming and work with it.

Carl Jung said, "We only gain merit and psychological development by accepting ourselves as we are and by being serious enough to live the lives we are entrusted with." My work was to integrate my feeling nature with the thinking nurture I had been given.

Feeling legitimized and empowered, I wanted to share this new piece of myself with Mother. Even after all these years, the mama's girl in me needed my mother's permission to feel my feelings and be allowed at the table as my natural self. I also longed to connect with her in the deeper way that I now knew was possible.

However, Mother was in a very different place. Since Dad's passing, she had further thrown herself into her job as administrator of the hospital. Despite her deteriorating health, she managed a large staff with the proverbial iron hand, now tougher than ever! Her excellent thinking and managerial skills had found their niche, and she was much celebrated in her position.

When I shared my new insights in the hopes of getting her to see and validate my feelings, past and present, I found Mother very reluctant to discuss emotions, even more so than before. Having experienced great success with her work, she continued to see things with her head. I, however, now empowered by the MBTI, dug in my heels and stayed with my new identity.

I found our weekly conversations difficult. Mother was her usual cheerful self, sharing anecdotes from her work or giving me the latest news in the lives of our extended family and friends. That was how we had spoken for years and years. But something had cracked open in me, and I now wanted more. I wanted to share with her the emptiness I was feeling. I wanted to know if she had ever experienced it. I needed her to tell me it was okay to feel this pain I had been feeling for months.

But Mother was uncomfortable being vulnerable. I, on the other hand, was uncomfortable *not* being vulnerable. As much as I adored her, I struggled to accept what I believed was her deliberate denial of my emotions. I spoke less and less and simply listened while she chatted. After each call, I hung up disappointed.

One day, I tried a new approach. I had recently come across an old picture of Mother as a newlywed. At eighteen, she looked so open and tender that it brought tears to my eyes. I imagined there was an inner child who could use some healing in her as well, and I decided to invite her on that journey with my own inner child.

I started our conversation over the phone that day by telling Mother about the photograph. Hoping for a deeper conversation, I wondered aloud where that young woman had gone. But that day, Mother had had enough. With a firm voice, she said, "That was then. This is now. That girl is no more. I have had to change and become this person to face the challenges life tossed my way. I have had to take up a career and learn new things to survive. We moved to a different part of the country, and I had to learn languages I was not raised with. I focused my energies on educating my three children and making sure they have a good life. I think I have done a tremendous job and am quite comfortable being who I am. I don't have any need to be who you think I should be. I have tried my best to be patient with you these past months, but now I am done. We will no longer discuss these emotional matters between us anymore. Take me or leave me as I am."

And that was that. I had to take her as she was and leave her where she had chosen to be.

And so, I did.

* * *

Although I did not quite realize it then, Mother was throwing me off the nest that we had both shared for years, one that I had already outgrown. I don't think she knew it either. Breakups of any nature are orchestrated by an intelligence far bigger than ours, and it was a gift. But it would take me a few more years to recognize it as such. Guruji had warned me that this was going to be my own journey. Yet for weeks, I lamented the door Mother had closed, feeling sorry for myself. Then, one day, something quite unrelated occurred that helped bring about a new perspective.

It was a bright weekend in December. It had been a snowy winter in Chicago, and we had just finished a heavy lunch. I was settling down on the couch for my little catnap when Krish walked in with the mail. There was the usual junk mail and a few year-end cards, most with the annual family picture. He was looking at the cards one by one when I heard him say, "Uh-oh, someone's in trouble!"

I asked him what was going on. With a puzzled expression on his face, Krish said, "I don't see Sean." One holiday card was missing a family member's name. "It must be a mistake," he went on.

Someone missed the name of a family member? I thought. *That is impossible.*

"Bring it here," I said, sitting up now. I looked at the card. Around the family picture in the center was printed, each in a distinct color, the name of every member. I read aloud, "Jake, Patti, Molly, Anna, Bruce, Sean, and Bud, their dog." They were all there. "They have four children, and they are all named. So is their dog. What's the problem?" I asked.

"I do not see Sean's name on the card," Krish said.

But there it was. I could see it clearly. "He is here." I pointed it out to Krish, wondering why he couldn't see what I was seeing.

"Where is it?" he asked.

I pointed to it again, tapping the spot firmly, now getting a little impatient.

He seemed to sense my annoyance rising as he kept insisting it was not there. "What color is it written in?" he asked me finally.

"A purple indigo."

"Ah, that's one my eyes do not get!"

I had forgotten about Krish's color blindness. His particular type of color blindness means his eyes cannot recognize a few shades, and this was one of them. I apologized to him and handed back the card.

The mystery of the missing name solved, I lay back on the couch but could not nap. I was remorseful about my earlier annoyance with Krish. He was unable to see, not because he did not want to but because he was unable to. How often in life do people respond from an internal disability, and how often do we realize it may not be intentional?

It brought me back to a similar frustration. Mother. My emotions were like the name "Sean" on that card. I wanted them to be seen by her. But what if human beings suffer from another kind of blindness—emotional blindness? One that has never been named as such?

The viewpoint of the MBTI and the *Gita* about essential human differences was getting through to me. Natural traits need to be worked with as a given. Like Krish with his color blindness, Mother's reluctance to "see" was not personal at all.

I needed to let Mother Nature have her victory and accept that Mother and I had reached the outer limits of our relationship in this area. In fact, by refusing to discuss emotions with me anymore, Mother had given me the gift of taking away the training wheels that had made me lean on her approval all my life. I did not need permission from her or anyone else to be myself. It was my job to accept my brand of humanity and become the best version of me.

As I journaled for days about the Christmas card episode, it occurred to me that blindness runs both ways. It is not only the thinkers who refuse to see the feelers. Feelers don't appreciate the thinkers either. I had called Mother countless times during difficult situations. Although she dismissed my feelings, she was a powerful fixer-doer, always coming up with great solutions or suggestions. In recent years, with my emotions at the forefront of my mind, I, too, had overlooked her strengths and her ability to deal with situations pragmatically.

The problem is never our differences. It is in attaching to our way of seeing, understanding, and interpreting the world, making an identity of our traits and believing our way to be the only right way.

My reflections brought me again to the story "The Three Little Pigs." Each of us, holding on to our natural inclinations, seeks to build safety around us. Yet neither thinker nor feeler had found a permanent and lasting way to keep away the wolf of adversity. Authentic power does not come with any one personality type but belongs to the one who is aware of, yet enjoys, freedom from these limiting identities.

I wanted to feel or think. And I wanted the freedom to choose either or both. The poet Rumi wrote these words:

Out beyond ideas of wrongdoing and rightdoing,

There is a field. I'll meet you there.

With his words in mind, I wrote in my journal, "Beyond all thinking and all feeling, there is a field. I am heading there."

CHAPTER REFLECTIONS

1. Continuing to work with the MBTI helped me shift the way I saw Mother's unique strengths and limitations. I finally accepted that there was only so much she could do for me. In which relationship in your life can you apply this wisdom and accept another for who they are and what they can (or cannot) bring to your life?

2. Read up about your particular MBTI type and about others who share your type (https://www.myersbriggs.org/). Although there are many others with your type, there is no one just like you. Reflect on how best to utilize your strengths and work with your shortcomings. Moving away from shame and guilt, inspire yourself to become the best version of your unique self. You owe it to your inner child!

3. Whatever your type, can you lean into the opposite side of it? If you identify as a thinker, can you lean into your feelings? If you identify as a feeler, try putting on your thinking hat and look at things from another angle.

CHAPTER 12

FEAR, THE FIRST RESPONDER

INSIGHT #10
*Fear can be our first responder, but it is
faith that needs to have the last word.*

I WOKE UP AND CHECKED the weather within. It was the same as every day: dark and filled with dread, as if some part of me already knew today was going to be awful. Although the inner work I had done had shifted my waking hours a great deal, somehow, the nighttime set things back, leaving me to start over every day. I reminded myself I had classes to teach that morning and drew myself up from under the covers.

Ironically, my business had started to improve. More students were coming my way even as clouds of diffidence continued to darken my inner climate. I had often joked that my students were following me at their own risk, but by some miraculous force, they did not seem to mind.

Wondering how many more years the dark ages of my life would continue, I came down the stairs, went into the kitchen, and began my usual process of making morning coffee. My hands knew where to reach for the special filter, a precious possession from my South Indian background.

The north and the south in India are like two different cultures, just as they are in the US. Tea estates lie in the north, making North Indians avid chai lovers. Coffee, on the other hand, is grown in plantations in the south. South Indians boast of their mastery in making coffee with their stainless-steel coffee filters.

My hands found the coffee container, then my fingers automatically spooned the right amount of ground coffee into the dripper and pressed it well for a strong dose. The water bubbled and whined while I poured it into the filter and then warmed the milk. The aroma in my kitchen brought back sweet memories of my younger self sitting groggy-eyed on the floor of Mother's kitchen. She was up every morning at four thirty, and by the time I woke at six thirty, she had finished most of her morning chores. With her usual cheerfulness, she would make me my morning coffee, following the same steps I now followed. I had watched her skilled hands make my drink hundreds of times.

Ten minutes later, I settled into my couch, hot coffee in hand. As I sipped the familiar beverage, part of me sat back and reviewed the scene, fascinated. I could have concocted that cup of coffee blindfolded. In fact, in a sense, I did. Every morning. My body, my mind, my fingers—every part of me—knew how to take me from the moment I opened my eyes to that first sip of coffee, with no conscious participation on my part.

It was not only coffee I could make blindfolded. Mother had initiated me into cooking when I was just twelve. I could now make a whole meal on autopilot, except for the most difficult part—choosing the day's menu! The way we can accomplish things without the conscious exercise of our free will is called muscle memory. Funny how we then claim credit or guilt for how it turns out.

I pondered muscle memory, wondering if it applies to our emotions as well. Do we have emotional muscle memory? Just as our physical muscles work from habit, do our emotional muscles also remember emotional habits? Are emotional reactions even based in our present reality? Or are they just on autopilot from the past?

My prolonged emptiness had led me to read more about emotions and their roots. Feeling like a detective, I approached the investigation from various angles, both Western and Eastern, hoping to crack the code and solve the mystery of my missing cheer.

All my reading, research, and reflection revealed one principal culprit—fear. Every discontent, every distress has its roots in fear—fear that lies dormant and surfaces from time to time, triggered by something in the external or internal environment.

One scientific study I read about, conducted by James V. McConnell, an assistant professor of psychology at the University of Michigan, gave me a powerful understanding of the far-reaching ripples of fear and its effects on all creatures, not just humans.

It was an experiment on two cans of live worms.

With the first can, the experimenters shined a bright light on the worms and immediately followed it with a mild electric shock. The worms bunched into a coil in response to the unpleasant experience. Scientists repeated the sequence—bright light followed by electric shock—until the worms had established a cause-and-effect connection in their little brains. Now the experimenters simply had to shine the light, and the worms would bunch themselves up into a coil in anticipation of the upcoming trauma.

At this stage, the scientists, attempting to study the mind-body connection, mashed up the first can of worms and fed them to the second can of worms.

Although this grossed me out, I was intrigued and continued to read. They then subjected the second can of worms to the bright light. The worms spontaneously cringed into a coil, even without the experience of the electric shock!

This was mind-blowing.

In fact, this secondhand experience of fear is true even for human beings. Epigenetics is the study of how trauma can change the way our DNA is expressed, reverberating down the line. The impact of events in a person's lifetime does get passed on to the next generation.

I wondered if we can ever really know where our fears come from. Are we the first can of worms, experiencing fear from a real cause in the world outside, or are we the second can of worms, experiencing an emotional memory passed down to us? Or maybe we are the third or the fourth can of worms. How many generations ago did the original traumatic event take place? Are we all suffering from multigenerational PTSD in one form or another?

Epigenetics answered questions I had long asked: Why do two people going through the same experience react or recover so differently? Are some simply more resilient than others?

I had posed these questions to the elders around me. They all had the same response: karma. That one word was supposed to put an end to the inquiry. I was not satisfied, but that was all I got, and I had to accept it.

But now, years later, all this research was shedding light on those questions.

If two children were to fall and scrape their knee, but one already had an injury in the same place, which child would hurt more and take longer to recover? Clearly the child with the earlier injury. Yet most cultures have concrete assumptions about how much a single wound is supposed to hurt and how much time it needs to heal. But how could anyone determine the journey toward healing without the knowledge of what exactly was being healed?

Applying this insight to emotions, we know that every person is carrying wounds from their family's history. These past wounds leave them vulnerable in certain areas, which is why each person has different sensitivities. When we feel more intensely than an event calls for, there is probably more to the wound than meets the eye. I began to refer to this as our "preexisting emotional condition"—the deeper traces of old trauma that we may not have experienced firsthand but whose aftermath lives in us.

So the elders were right after all. That was karma indeed—a mysterious cause with roots in the past.

The scientific understanding of trauma being passed down through generations resembles the Eastern concept of karma flowing down from our ancestors. But the *Gita* has an additional piece of wisdom that sets the two views apart.

Science looks at trauma and its impact on the individual from the outside in. If someone suffers from ill health or a difficult upbringing, it is the unfortunate accident of being born in the wrong family. We are the passive victims.

According to the *Gita*, birth is not a random event but an intentional choice made by a deeper self, our soul. Our soul chooses experiences that enable us to learn and embody qualities such as compassion, kindness, courage, and so on. According to this perspective, we are the cause, and the families we are born into are the effect.

The *Gita* sees our life on Earth as an evolutionary journey, each lifetime merely one page, with growth being the end. Depending on how much progress we make during a lifetime, we pick a family in the next one. Therefore, the pain caused by ill health or a difficult upbringing is seen as an opportunity manifested by the soul to learn and grow in and through such experiences.

As I sat there with my coffee cup, I heard the alarm go off in my son's room, interrupting my reverie. Anish had an early morning session at school for his violin performance. I had sat with my reflections for over an hour, my cup long empty. I had begun the morning's ruminations on muscle memory, applying it to emotional muscles, remembering the worms, and wondering if my emotional pain was the result of some inherited trauma, then brought in the teachings of the *Gita* to see all of my experiences as choices I had made at a soul-ular level.

I wrapped up the morning's meanderings with the conclusion that I needed to practice new responses. That was the only way to create a new muscle memory—physical and emotional. Or, in the language of my upbringing, only then could I start a new karmic cycle.

*　*　*

The next morning, although I woke up with my now regular morning blues, I approached my inner work with a new awareness and inspiration. Looking within my huddle, I recognized the face of fear behind many of the stuck emotions: worry, envy, anger, shame. No matter their faces or stories, I realized fear was in each of them.

This ubiquity of fear reminded me of a powerful story from Hindu mythology about Goddess Durga, an aspect of the divine feminine worshiped widely in India. I was introduced to goddess worship early in my childhood, and many stories from its rich and colorful mythology still lived in me, coming up from time to time.

The word *durga* means "invincible" or, literally, "unpassable." The Goddess Durga is the courageous slayer of fear. In the legend, she appears on Earth to help save humans from the horrors of the buffalo demon Mahishasura. As Durga appears on the battlefield, riding strong and tall upon a ferocious lion ("her crown scraping the sky, her strong feet on the Earth"), Mahishasura is terrified by the sight. He changes form to fool her, appearing as a man, then appearing as a bull, then as an elephant, and on and on. At first, Durga is gentle, destroying one form at a time. Then, realizing this could be an endless battle, she decides to put an end to his antics.

Taking a powerful breath, the Goddess rises above all the different forms to see the single demon in all of them, slaying him once and for all. When all is still, his slain form before her, his consciousness returns to the Goddess, attaining union with her again. He was always an emanation of *her*, from *her*.

The story reminded me that the demon of fear lives in everyone and assumes different forms. What is worse is that in all its various forms, fear is convincing. We tend to buy into its stories and react without realizing (as the experiment with the worms shows us) that what we feel is not always true. There is a reason for this—nature has wired us with a negativity bias. Our systems are set up to be more sensitive to a negative situation than to a neutral or even a positive one. When confronted by a negative scenario, this wiring generates chemicals three times stronger than our emotions in neutral scenarios. Because of this bias, negative stories feel more compelling; we spontaneously go into a self-protective fight-or-flight mode.

But blindly believing in our automatically generated fear alarms can be dangerous. If not checked, our animal instincts become like the demons that Goddess Durga is called upon to slay.

It was time to distance myself from the loyalty I was feeling to the scared faces in my huddle and the stories they each carried. Through my months of letter writing and journaling, I had addressed the past. From my study of the MBTI, I had come to understand that I couldn't help feeling deeply about everything. All I could do now was teach myself to respond differently.

I wondered, *What if I interpreted the divine intervention of Durga as the intervention I needed to make when my fear-based first responder released a blast of uncomfortable emotions?*

Taking a deep breath, I invoked Durga's presence. She was the strong side of the divine feminine, the one who overcame fear with wisdom and courage. I needed to embody her strength and awareness to take my power back from my first responders and move toward health and healing.

CHAPTER REFLECTIONS

1. Take an honest look at the emotions that hold you down. Can you see the fear beneath their stories and beliefs? What are these fears? Can you give them a name?

2. How old are these fears/beliefs? Journal about them to see when and how you picked them up. Explore their roots to see if they are multigenerational.

3. Step aside and watch your fears in an unbiased way to strengthen the Goddess Durga in you. Let the old stories in your huddle play themselves out as you simply breathe and listen. Every time you find yourself defending or analyzing your stories, take a slow breath, drop the story, and return to your Durga self. Do this every day for at least five to seven minutes.

CHAPTER 13

SEVEN AND A HALF YEARS TO SURRENDER

INSIGHT #11

Rituals done with intention can help cultivate faith and resilience.

USHA WAS IN THE driver's seat as we left the city of Bangalore for a bumpy ride over muddy roads to meet Hari, her friend and favorite astrologer. I had been in India for the past few days, my first visit since Dad had passed over a year earlier. On this afternoon, Usha and I had been relaxing with our mother after an amazing lunch. Mother had surpassed herself with an even more delicious meal than usual, including some of my favorite dishes. We lay together, all three of us, on our parents' king-size bed, chatting.

All my life, I had seen my mother and sister as more positive and resilient than me, maybe because I was the youngest child. While I was feeling stronger and wiser this day than on my previous visit, I was still making my way through my inner battles and outer challenges. I was sharing some of my struggles when Usha jumped up in her typical way and said, "I know what. Let's go meet Hari. He will surely have some good advice for you."

Hari. It had been a while since I'd heard that name. Hari was a Vedic astrologer. Like Western astrology, Vedic astrology is based on the belief that the planets and other heavenly bodies influence a person's life. I remembered my meeting with Hari several years earlier. During a reading of my natal chart (a map of the skies at the time of my birth), he had described me and my life with such amazing precision that I looked askance at Usha. *Did she tip him off?* She shrugged and shook her head.

"Will Hari be free today?" I wondered aloud now.

Usha made a quick call. Yes, Hari was available and happy to meet us for a consult. Usha was confident we would be back in a few hours and in time for dinner. So the two of us set off right away.

I was excited, hoping for some favorable predictions.

Hari lived miles away from the heart of the city and seemed to enjoy the seclusion. By making his home in this remote place, he had made it difficult for people to visit him, perhaps intentionally.

"Hello, Ramaa Madam," he said as we entered, inviting us to sit. Addressing a person with a respectful suffix is an old and common practice in India. In recent times, people had become more informal, but Hari insisted on this manner of speech.

"It's been so long, Hari," I said.

"Yes, madam. Eight years."

We settled into comfortable cane chairs around a wooden center table in his cozy little living room.

"Ramaa has been going through some really tough times," Usha began. "Would you take a look and tell us what is going on?"

"Yes, of course. I am already on it." Hari pointed to his laptop on the table. "I pulled up her birth information from my old files."

"So, what's going on, Hari?" Usha asked as I sat back and listened, grateful to have Usha playing big sister.

"Well, Ramaa Madam is in the middle of her sade sati. That's what's going on," Hari replied.

"Oh!" Usha and I jointly let out a sound of dismay. We all knew what that meant and became quiet.

Sade sati (meaning "seven and a half" in Hindi) is a period of seven and a half years when, according to the ancient Indian astrological system, a person is in the grip of the planet Saturn. This happens once in a thirty-year cycle. It is understood to be a testing time, and no human being is spared. However, the intensity depends on the placement of the planets in each case.

I remembered when I had heard about sade sati for the first time. It was shortly after my exam failure at nineteen. A friend of the family had recommended we consult an astrologer for my "misfortune," and Mother had taken me to someone. It was then that we learned I was right in the midst of Saturn's testing period. Although it was a very difficult time, it was thanks to that journey that I met my first spiritual teacher and received the lifelong gift of meditation.

And now I was back.

"How many more years, Hari?" I asked, even as I started tracing the history of my recent struggles.

"Four."

Four more years? I wanted to get up and leave right then, but Hari's wife entered the room with a tray in her hand. Knowing that walking out would be rude, I settled down and smiled at her.

"Hello, Usha Madam, Ramaa Madam," she said and placed the tray in the center. There were also cups of filtered coffee along with some savory snacks. A welcome break. We reached for our coffees and chatted with his wife for a while. Then she left the room to let us continue.

Usha moved the conversation forward. "So, what should she do, Hari?"

"Well, Ramaa Madam is a little tough, not like you, Usha Madam." He laughed in a friendly way, but I glared at him.

"She will not give up. It's an old problem with her," he went on, describing many astrological combinations in my chart that made me a "tough customer."

I knew he was referring to my relentless quest for success. Even when I had first met him all those years ago, he had said that the secret to my happiness was to work less, not more.

Usha nodded and seemed to say, "Tell me about it."

"I think not giving up is a good thing," I said in my defense.

"Yes, it is. At other times," Hari replied. "But not during sade sati. Saturn is the Lord of Boundaries. He is here to teach us the limits of our ego. The more you resist, the more difficult he makes it."

"So what am I supposed to do? Just sit and be miserable?"

I had come here looking for good news, but he was offering me no hope. In fact, he had made it worse. This whole visit had been a bad idea. Four more years! I began to weep.

"No, please don't cry, madam," Hari said. "Saturn is like a teacher on a mission. He wishes you to learn and grow."

"Learn and grow? What else have I been doing all my life?" I railed.

"Yes, I know, but you don't understand. Saturn is also a healer. If you work with him, he will bless you with gifts beyond what you expect." Hari went on. "If you go with the flow, it will not be so bad. And then there are some upaayaas I will tell you about. You will definitely find relief."

Upaayaas are the therapeutic rituals and remedial practices integral to Indian astrology. I pulled myself together and reminded myself not to shoot the messenger.

I took a deep breath. "I'm sorry I lost it," I said. "Please tell me what I can do to make it easier on myself."

"There are many things you can do. Our astrological system recognizes planets as live energies you can influence and interact with. These upaayaas are aimed toward befriending the malefic forces, trusting the experiences that land in your lap, particularly the difficult ones. One of the things that will help you is buying a small image of a snake and worshipping it every day."

"A snake?" I was horrified.

"Yes," he said. "The snake is a symbol of all that you fear. When you befriend your fears, you can work with them instead of feeling threatened by them."

"Befriend our fears? I thought we had to face and overcome them just like Goddess Durga conquered Mahishasura," I responded, knowing he was familiar with the story.

"Ah, yes. Good question!" replied Hari. "But there is one big difference. Durga was not afraid of Mahishasura. She simply dealt with him as she needed to. True resilience means you do what you have to on the outside while remaining centered within."

He was right. Despite all my inner work, at my core, I still feared adversity.

"All right," I conceded, letting out a big sigh. I had been hoping Hari would give me some relief with his predictions. I had not expected him to add to my already crowded to-do list in the self-care department.

He looked at Usha and gave her some instructions on where to procure the image of the snake for me.

Then he continued. "Another thing. There is a great book you need to read. It is an ancient story that is now available in a very good English translation, *The Greatness of Saturn*, by Robert Svoboda."

I had read other books by the author and had profound respect for his work. So I decided that part should be easy. I looked forward to reading it, although I didn't know what he meant by a "therapeutic story."

Before we left, Hari suggested that I pray chants, offer items to Saturn, and donate to the poor and needy to find some relief. I was returning to the US the following day, but thanks to Hari's list, I had some shopping to do.

On our way back, Usha and I discussed Hari's findings. I also told her of Guruji's warning that I would be going through tough times, and we pieced it together. Clearly, this period was a part of my soul's plan. My conversation with Guruji happened four years earlier. The idea of four more years was a heavy one to hold. I was tired and shared my feelings with my sister.

Usha sympathized while advising me to follow Hari's recommendations. "I know you like to study science, psychology, and genetics and such, but the ancient Hindus knew a thing or two as well, you know. It is a different approach, but it works for millions on this side of the planet. So, you need to give it a try," she said. There was often a little rivalry between us over the new things I was learning outside India while Usha delved deeper into the spiritual wisdom of our birthland.

"Well, Carl Jung himself believed in the power of ancient rituals to heal. He would approve of this move," I joked.

We bought the image of an Indian cobra in silver. This snake is known and feared for its venom, which is powerful enough to kill. My knee-jerk reaction to Hari's suggestion had since settled, and I was approaching the ritual with a new respect.

I grew up watching people worship snakes—both real ones and idols in our temples—but always viewed it as a superstitious practice followed by blind believers. Over my years of travel, though, I had come across depictions of snakes and dragons in other cultures as well. Thanks to my studies at the Jung Institute, I could now see the snake as a symbol of something deeper in the human psyche.

We also stopped by the bookstore to buy Svoboda's *The Greatness of Saturn* before returning home to Mother, who eagerly awaited our report on our visit with Hari.

* * *

Back in the US, I completed my first reading of *The Greatness of Saturn*. Hari had described it as a "therapeutic story," and I had imagined that simply reading it would result in magical healing. But a quick read from cover to cover did not do anything for me. While it was no doubt very well written, I didn't know how it applied to my life and struggles. I called Usha and let her know it had not worked. Her response was prompt and brief.

"Well, then read it again, and keep reading it until it does!"

I returned to the book, more patiently this time. Usha was correct in her guidance. Gradually, the tale broke through my walls and began to speak volumes to me.

The story is about a noble king, Vikramaditya. An astrologer warns him that he is about to enter the seven-and-a-half-year period of Saturn. Soon thereafter, the king, while riding a new horse (who is influenced by Saturn), lands in a kingdom far, far away. There, owing to a series of unfortunate events, he is accused of theft and thrown into prison. Punishment follows a quick trial, and, per the law of that land, his arms and legs are publicly amputated. Realizing that he is being tested by Saturn, the king accepts his fate even as he writhes in pain. A passerby, who happens to be a visitor from Vikramaditya's own kingdom, recognizes him and offers to help the miserable king. Vikramaditya asks the man to find him a safe place to live.

His sympathizer happens to be related to the owner of an oil mill, who employs the king to sit upon his oil press as it spins round and round, his physical weight doing all the work needed. In return, the king is given shelter and care.

Although extremely distraught at first, the king begins finding peace and healing within himself. As the years pass, he begins to sing in joy and gratitude. His sweet music reaches far and wide, all the way to the ears of the princess, the daughter of the king of this foreign land. Curious to meet the one whose music is creating the magic within the kingdom, she finds her way to Vikramaditya. The princess proceeds to fall in love with him, declaring to her father that she will marry none but the limbless musician. Though not completely happy over this, the king agrees to their union.

The night before the wedding, Saturn appears in a dream to the soon-to-be groom. The seven and a half years have ended. Expressing his pleasure over how gracefully the king handled his adversity, Saturn asks him to make a wish. Vikramaditya knows exactly what he wants. He requests Saturn to spare everyone else from the kind of pain inflicted upon him. Impressed by his unselfishness, Saturn rewards him by returning his limbs.

The next morning, the wedding takes place, and the bride and groom return to Vikramaditya's kingdom, where his return is celebrated.

As I read the story more intentionally, I understood the metaphor. The king's horse taking him out of his kingdom was the hand of Saturn taking us out of our comfort zones during the seven-and-a-half-year test. That transition to a foreign land could occur through an external shift, an internal shift, or both. I myself had moved out of teaching from my home to my new studio at the start of my sade sati. Not a businesswoman, I had felt like a stranger in a strange land, even living among the people who knew and loved me.

The amputated arms and legs represent the feeling that there is nothing one can do and no place one can go. It is a time of no escape. Like the king who let the weight of his body do the work, we may only have the ability to lean into the power of our own authentic presence. Having nowhere to go and accepting what is, we can find peace and, finally, our unique voice. The end of the story was the assurance I badly needed for my own life—things were not merely restored to normal. They were even better.

In light of my reading, I reviewed where I was on my own journey. Clearly,

I was no Vikramaditya. Encountering Elizabeth Lesser's wisdom on the inevitability of suffering some months earlier, I had no doubt shifted from resistance to acceptance, but my acceptance was not like that of the noble king. Although I had made some progress with my need to fix things, it had returned beneath different masks. My research, meditation, dreamwork, journaling, and analysis had become my new ways of control, my new attempt to safeguard against adversity.

Two steps forward, one step back.

The fact that the king, even upon being recognized by someone from his country, did not attempt to be rescued but chose to go through his sade sati was a point that caught my attention. Knowing he was in Saturn's grip, Vikramaditya had decided to surrender to the transformative experiences coming his way.

Hari had described me as a tough customer, and he was right. I had moved from resistance to acceptance but still did not trust the journey. Acceptance without trust is resignation, a place of passive victimhood. Acceptance combined with trust is a surrender that opens up the hidden possibilities in ourselves and our situations.

The message of surrender was suddenly speaking to me everywhere. Every time I opened the *Gita*, I seemed to land at the same theme:

> Knowledge is better than practice; meditation is better than knowledge; and best of all is surrender, which soon brings peace.
> The resolute in yoga surrender results, and gain perfect peace; the irresolute, attached to results, are bound by everything they do.

I came across this same message of surrender in the Bible too: "But I tell you, don't resist him who is evil; but whoever strikes you on your right cheek, turn to him the other also."

I added the snake worship as part two of my morning routine. Part one included my morning coffee, meditation, and journaling. Then later, after eating breakfast and sending everyone off, I would reach for the little silver cobra Usha and I had bought.

Traditional worship of idols is quite elaborate, involving bathing the deities in milk and water and offering incense, flowers, fruit, and all kinds of food preparations. But Usha had given me a simpler regimen: Light a lamp or a candle, bathe the snake with milk and then water, wipe the image dry, and replace it at the altar. Then bathe it with the scented wafts from incense sticks and end the worship with a few minutes of quiet prayer and silence.

Each day, I prayed for the serenity to accept and trust that which could not be changed. It took me no more than seven minutes, but the ritual brought me great peace. It was my final practice before leaving for my day at the studio.

As I continued with my daily worship, the work I had done with Jackie on decoding dream symbols was coming back. The venomous cobras lurking beneath the surface represented the unconscious fears "under the ground" of the psyche—the fear of trauma from multiple generations as well as the fear of our own feelings and urges that make us so uncomfortable that we want to push them down. Carl Jung referred to these as our shadow.

Through *The Greatness of Saturn*, I was learning to surrender and finally allowing my journey to mold me. Although I did not understand how it worked, by remaining still and allowing the experience, I was being transformed—just like those seven caterpillars on my blanket.

CHAPTER REFLECTIONS

1. Rituals are an important part of our self-care routine and are the bridge between our inner and outer worlds. There are many rituals—some simple and some more elaborate—performed daily, weekly, or even yearly. What do you need at this time in your life? Consider adopting a ritual and allowing its magic to unfold.

2. Reflect on the rituals from your faith tradition or heritage to see which ones speak to you. You can also create one of your own. It can be simple—even watering your garden or walking mindfully around your favorite tree could be your ritual. Build your routine around it and do it regularly, even if only for a few minutes per day, setting aside all other distractions. Make sure to engage in your ritual from a place of love and surrender—not from a place of fear and guilt. If you miss a day, let it go. Don't beat yourself up about it.

PART 4

DEEPENING

CHAPTER 14

INTERBEING IN THE WORLD WIDE WEB

INSIGHT #12

People in our trigger-view mirror are closer to us than they appear.

I WAS SOON BACK TO my everyday struggles in the US, where life felt like a battlefield and my enemies were my friends on Facebook. With unerring accuracy, their posts seemed to target where I was hurting on any day. If I was struggling with my teenagers, I would see a post from one of my friends lauding her amazing teen. If I was tired of my husband's travels, there would be a post about how a doting husband had sent roses. On a day that my class offerings had no takers, someone posted about their extremely successful project. My lament of the day was their victory post.

The matter came up at lunch one day with a group of close friends who were part of the community I had built. We had been studying together for many years. I had recently had a birthday, and we were celebrating it at my favorite Indian restaurant on Devon Avenue. We were waiting for our cups of chai to finish off our delicious meal when I began unwrapping my gifts. A laminated poster from Peggy stood out to me. It read, "I will not compare myself to strangers on the Internet."

I chuckled and said, "You know me well! Just what I needed!"

I went on to share about the cruel synchronicity I was experiencing lately, regaling my captive audience with my various Facebook anecdotes.

"The very thing that I am upset about, I see somebody enjoying online, flaunting it even. Every time. There's surely a force taunting me, and it wants me to feel bad. How does this happen?" I said, unfolding the conspiracy theory I was conjuring.

"Don't forget you are in your seven-and-a-half," Veronique said wisely.

Having been deeply touched by Robert Svoboda's *The Greatness of Saturn*, I now led study groups to reflect on its wisdom, applying it to situations we had no escape from. All the ladies at lunch that day had been part of the Saturn study group.

"Yes, draw the gold from the filth," Katie added, reminding me of a quote by Jung as the waiter brought us our cups of chai.

I shook my head in disbelief over my predicament but added, "Yes, I believe that Jungian quote actually came from a Latin phrase that translates to 'That which you most need will be found where you least want to look.'"

"Okay then, dear friend." Sharon pretended to raise a toast with her cup of chai. "Here's to another year of digging around in the filth. May you come up with a treasure!"

"And share it with us all," Bridget added.

Amidst our laughter, I gathered up my gifts, grateful for friends I could share my woes with.

* * *

Back home, I was still thinking of our lunch conversation as I looked for the right place to display Peggy's gift. It was a piece of wisdom I wanted to keep handy. We had moved into our new home a year earlier, and I had claimed a room in the basement for my inner work. It was my personal "kitchen and pantry," where I meditated, journaled, read, and cooked up my day. I decorated it with a chart of the chakras, pictures of some of my favorite teachers, and images from various faith traditions. Bookshelves, along with a comfortable recliner, completed my safe haven, where I spent hours each day.

While hanging up my new poster, I spotted a book that seemed to intentionally catch my attention, the way books sometimes do. It was Pema Chödrön's *The Places That Scare You*, a gift from my dear late friend Nancy. I had meditated with her during her struggles with a brain tumor, and she had given me this book as a token of appreciation. At the time, I had been put off by the title, thinking it was "too negative."

That was years ago. Nancy had since died, and while I thought of her often, I had entirely forgotten about this book. I stared at it now, surprised. It sat tucked away in a corner until this moment, when it suddenly seemed to have jumped out.

As they say, when a student is ready, the teacher arrives. The teacher may be alive or dead, in person or in a book. One way or another, the teachings arrive when it is time.

I began reading the book.

The Places That Scare You is not a book about places on the outside but places within us, and it compels a reader to take a good look at what lies beneath those uncomfortable emotions we all want to run away from.

In recent days, seeing myself as King Vikramaditya from *The Greatness of Saturn*, I was learning to surrender and be transformed by the difficult situations in my life. Now I was ready to gather some new teachings and tools to help me face my fears.

Pema Chödrön is a Buddhist nun, and her wisdom comes from that tradition. Although Buddhism and the teachings of the *Gita* share many parallels, Buddhism has a very different focus. Hinduism is the older of the two religions. Gautam Buddha, the founder of Buddhism, was born a Hindu who, in reinterpreting the teachings and adding his own insights, began a new path—in the same way Jesus Christ, born into the Jewish faith, founded Christianity.

The teachings of Buddhism are built on a fundamental premise: all human experiences are impermanent, and human suffering is a consequence of resisting that impermanence. The importance of accepting the essential fluidity of life, instead of constantly seeking stability and permanence, is the core message of *The Places That Scare You*.

From my recent learnings, I now saw Buddhism in a new light. It did not have a pessimistic outlook but a deeply compassionate and empowering one. I likened it to exposure therapy in Western psychology, which involves exposing a patient to the source of their anxiety to help them confront their fears. Only this was spiritual exposure therapy. By inviting us to face our fears from a safe place, the practices move us beyond resistance to the possibilities within every situation.

Saturn had been revealing my fears no matter where I looked, so this was the perfect book for me, and I read it several times. Then I wanted more deep wisdom and gentle humor from Chödrön (or Ani Pema, as she is addressed). The next book I read was *Comfortable with Uncertainty*. This one stayed on my personal bestseller list for many years.

The opening words of *Comfortable with Uncertainty: 108 Teachings on Cultivating Fearlessness and Compassion* warmed my heart: "Spiritual awakening is frequently described as a journey to the top of a mountain. We leave our attachments and our worldliness behind and slowly make our way to the top. At the peak we have transcended all pain."

Indeed.

I had seen the spiritual journey as an ascent to the top. The *Gita* says the human journey is not the same for everyone, but I had understood that to mean we all ascend differently, imagining that some may climb on foot, some on a horse, others in an elevator. But we always journey in one direction. Upward.

After my first big dream with the little girl in red, I continued to have many vivid dreams. One theme in particular came up often. I would see myself going down—sometimes down a slide of water, sometimes down a mountain—but always down. Despite Jackie's assurances, I had been a little worried this was a warning sign that my life itself was going down.

But Ani Pema went on: "The only problem with this metaphor is that we leave all others behind. Their suffering continues, unrelieved by our personal escape."

I had never thought of spiritual growth as a personal escape. And, of course, it had not included others and their suffering. Now my brand of spirituality felt selfish. I read further:

On the journey of the warrior-bodhisattva, the path goes down, not up, as if the mountain pointed toward the earth instead of the sky. Instead of transcending the suffering of all creatures, we move toward turbulence and doubt however we can. We explore the reality and unpredictability of insecurity and pain, and we try not to push it away. If it takes years, it takes lifetimes, we let it be as it is . . . we move down and down . . . Right down there in the thick of things, we discover the love that will not die.

There it was—the journey downward. To face, not to flee. I saw in this teaching the third little pig, who did not deny, avoid, escape, or surrender to the wolf's hunger. It surrendered to the *inevitability* of the wolf in the jungle, yes, but then prepared to face it. I reinterpreted the dream of going down as going deeper, and the idea of internally readying myself for difficult situations no longer felt negative.

Triggering or upsetting events will always be a part of life. Freedom does not mean finding a perfect life but arriving at a place in myself where I no longer *need* perfection. My perfectly imperfect self lives in a perfectly imperfect world. I was on a path of learning how to respond to life's uncertainty in the best ways I could.

Within me, Ani Pema's books were connecting powerful perspectives between spiritual theory and human reality. For the first time, I was learning how to consciously integrate anger, despair, envy, and so on with the spiritual goals of being kind, honest, and helpful.

Another Buddhist teacher whose works drew me in was the great mindfulness master Thich Nhat Hanh, or Thay, as he was fondly known. I found myself adding new words and ideas to my spiritual vocabulary.

One particularly impactful concept was expressed through the word *interbeing*, as introduced by Thay.

Interbeing is the relationship between an individual and the collective. The teaching of interbeing states that, like the ocean and its wave—which look separate but are both basically the same water—our individual differences express a single consciousness. No individual life or story stands on its own. Even when we feel alone, we are not isolated beings, but interbeings. Meaning, we are the water, which is both the wave and the ocean. What we feel comes from the shared waters of our interbeing, and our responses feed it. Thus, we affect each other all the time. Our problems, both personal and collective, are born out of our failure to see our interconnectedness, and their solutions lie in correcting our vision.

With this understanding of interbeing, I viewed my experiences on Facebook differently. There was no Universe vs. me conspiracy or a karmic payback at play. I embraced a new interpretation of the synchronistic Facebook posts. We were all in this together.

As a mother attached to the successes and defeats of her children and as the owner of a business attached to the success of that business, I was in the same corner of the ocean as others who shared these very attachments. This was the common thread between us. While they reveled in their successes, I wallowed in my defeats. It's like we were on the same seesaw together, but they were on the high end while I was on the low end, my feet in the dirt. One person getting off the seesaw would be a game changer for everybody. If I could overcome my attachment to success, I could free my counterparts on the other end as well so we could all move on from the seesaw to a game less polarizing and more uniting.

Aspiring for success is healthy and different from an attachment to it. Attachment is a love of something coupled with the fear of losing it, as if it holds one's identity. The more triggered I was by a post, the greater my attachment to something. Triggers are neither punitive dead-ends nor invitations to self-improvement. They are opportunities to look deeper, beyond the camouflage our stories provide.

Each trigger was my invitation, my cue, to recognize the fear behind it and let it go. To choose opening up over shutting down. And by making that choice, I would change the energy in our corner of the ocean, making it easier for everyone else to release their own fears.

Thich Nhat Hanh's book *No Mud, No Lotus: The Art of Transforming Suffering* illustrates how a lotus—a sacred flower symbolizing purity and strength—cannot grow in marble. It needs the mud. So, too, do we need the messiness of life to bloom. To bloom is to open up to a freer, more expansive version of ourselves. But blooming is a choice. When faced with our old fears, we could shrink and descend into our old narratives and reactions or use them as opportunities to rise.

I decided to strengthen myself to face my challenges. There were several exercises laid out in the books written by Pema Chodron and Thich Nhat Hanh, which I now began to practice regularly.

I called it the Yoga of self-love, and I created a little verse to cue myself when facing moments of fear:

It's just a feeling. Feel it and breathe it.

Breathe it, don't believe it.

Don't fight it. Don't fear it. Don't feed it. Don't fix it. Don't file it.

Feel it and free it.

Live it and leave it.

Bless it and bless you.

Bless your life and everyone else too.

There were easy days and difficult ones, but I was realizing that the only way to deal with the scary places in myself was to transform them.

CHAPTER REFLECTIONS

1. What are some things that scare you the most?

2. Triggers are signs of being attached to someone or something. Attachment is the love of something, along with the fear of losing it. How can you love with freedom, not fear-dom?

3. When triggered next time, pause, breathe, and relax. Take a close look at whatever or whoever you think is triggering you. See what you share in common with the one that upsets you. Take a mindful walk or breathe slowly to allow yourself to release your reaction and respond as needed. Inner strength is built one thoughtful response at a time.

CHAPTER 15

LEARNING OF THE EMOTIONAL TRIANGLE

INSIGHT #13
It takes two to tango but three to steady them.

AFTER A LONG AND unrelenting winter, we finally had a gorgeous spring day, and my friend Sharon and I were on a long walk, our first in many months. The snow had finally melted. As we made our way through our neighborhood park along the beach, I heard birds singing, watched squirrels scurrying merrily, and saw people everywhere celebrating the coming of the sun.

My conversations with Sharon were usually deep. She is a psychotherapist, trained from a Western perspective, but she had been studying the Eastern spiritual approach with me for many years. Our conversations often compared, contrasted, and combined these philosophies and methodologies. We shared the belief that all issues, both personal and global, are expressions of the consciousness within. Together, we would examine the issues weighing on our minds to explore the deeper messages beneath external events.

I was sharing with Sharon my recent insights about my experiences on Facebook and how they helped me see things differently.

"I'm really in a much better place now," I said. "Come to think of it, it has been many weeks since a post set me off."

"How come?" she asked.

"Well, I treat my time on Facebook as part of my inner work. I am not seeking pleasure but growth from the experience. When I am triggered by something, instead of judging or blaming others, I do the inner work, and it helps me find balance."

Sharon was happy for my progress. She had always been a little amused by how personally affected I was by social media.

"What exactly do you do in the moment?" she asked.

"I've come up with a nice set of steps. First, I accept the triggers instead of resisting or denying them. Then I ask myself what I am really afraid of and name my fears. Then I pause and breathe and apply what I call 'The Serenity Prayer Treatment' to it. That always makes me feel much better and respond appropriately."

"That's great, Rumster. Good for you!" Sharon cheered my efforts, using a variant of my name that she reserved for special moments. I had initially protested, saying that it rhymed with *dumpster*, but we were beyond that point now.

"The interesting thing is," I went on, "my experiences online have actually changed. It's like Wayne Dyer said, 'When you change the way you look at things, the things you look at change.' I'm having the same experience with Mother."

"Oh, good. I had been meaning to ask. How are things between you now?" asked Sharon.

"Much better. As I have been working on myself, things have really settled down between us. At least most of the time. Our relationship was also like that seesaw. The stronger I held on to my emotions, the stronger she got in denying her own. And having Usha has helped. Sometimes, she speaks up for me; sometimes, she is Mother's spokesperson. But we are all getting along nicely."

"Ah, yes. Emotional triangles." Sharon replied. "Such an integral part of every family."

I figured Sharon was referring to her knowledge and experience with the Bowen family systems theory. This theory views the family as an emotional unit and examines their various interactions as a system.

"Emotional triangles? Tell me more," I said, curious.

"Well, Murray Bowen, from his study of relationships, came to understand that the minimum number of people required for maintaining stability in relationships is three."

"Three? Not two?" I asked.

"That's right. Stress of any sort in a relationship between two people can cause conflict. Triangulating in the third deflects the stress."

"Like when we share with a friend or vent to a family member, you mean?" I asked.

"Certainly," Sharon went on. "But the third could also be a pet, a passion, a hobby, or even a situation such as health, weight, money, and so on. Focusing on the third shifts the attention away from the real stressor."

"I imagine the third plays the part of balancing the irregular distribution between the two on the seesaw," I offered.

"You could say that, although it is much more complex. And there may not be just one triangle but many whose function is to absorb anxiety and sustain the family system. Think of a family as a home whose bricks are triangles, not rectangles."

I knew that Carl Jung also believed the tension between opposites could be reconciled only by a third. "It is amazing how threes show up everywhere," I commented. "In every school of thought, in one form or another. I hadn't seen it applied to families and relationships though."

Sharon continued, clearly having thought of this. "Bowen says anxiety that remains unaddressed in the family system gets passed down from one generation to the next through blaming, avoiding, or even completely cutting off a family member rather than digging deeper to work on resolutions."

"So that is what's going on in our family? Mother and I are playing out the preexisting anxieties in our family system?"

"Yes, you could say that."

"And when did this start?"

"You would need to examine the multigenerational stories within your family. It may go back a couple of generations or more, the ripples of which you're feeling now."

"Wow! So, I am not the problem then?" I asked, needing to make sure.

"Not entirely, no. Nor is your mother. You happen to be sensitive and take things personally. She is tough and pragmatic, but neither of you is causing the problem. Unresolved and ongoing anxiety exists within a family and is frequently older than its current members. By making deep shifts within yourself, you could even be the catalyst that relieves the pressure within your family system."

I paused for a deep breath of fresh air, suddenly breathing in a whole new reality. I had always been the most sensitive one in my family. This meant I was like the canary in the coal mine, an indicator that there was emotional pain to address. I was not the problem, but maybe I could be the solution.

"And what would these deep internal shifts be?" I asked.

"Bowen called them the differentiation of self, which is a person recognizing their own thoughts and feelings and respecting how they are sometimes different from others."

I chewed on this for a bit, with many light bulbs turning on as I did so. I was making several connections simultaneously.

"The idea of differentiation sounds like Carl Jung's process of individuation and its impact on collective consciousness," I began. "And in the East, we talk about self-realization and how it can retire family karmic patterns. So many similarities between different traditions! But they all agree that our choices are impacted by the fears of our forefathers. Even the Bible talks about sons paying for their father's sins. Yet when something goes wrong or right in our lives, we blame or praise one single member without seeing the individual's behavior in the larger context of the family's history."

Sharon agreed. "That's why, as a family systems therapist, I always insist on looking at the larger picture instead of designating just one person as the black sheep of the family."

I was reminded of the story "The Princess and the Pea" and said, "Maybe the black sheep is just very sensitive to the anxious undercurrents and is acting out of that? Perhaps the black sheep is actually the white sheep?"

"I wouldn't go that far," Sharon replied. "Black sheep are not demons, but neither are they angels. But they can serve as a way for the system to deflect its chronic anxiety. The family focuses their anxiety on that one person and avoids dealing with their own issues. In fact, the black sheep could use the great opportunity to do some deep personal digging and come out healthier on the other end."

Sharon often spoke in terms of chronic anxiety, which I had come to understand as worrying, obsessing, or overreacting to life's situations over a prolonged period of time. It sounded like an individual problem. Now she was pointing out how the black sheep's behavior makes them the focus of blame and serves as a distraction from the system-wide issues. Chronic anxiety wasn't the fault of the black sheep alone. If the black sheep were to wake up, the entire system would have an opportunity to wake up as well.

"So, the black sheep can open up the possibility of relief for everyone in the family," I mused. This perspective was both new and relieving.

I thought of another thing. The *Gita* says that birth is not an accident but an intentional placement. Sharon had studied the *Gita* with me and knew about this. We had also recently read a book, suggested by one of the ladies in our community, called *Your Soul's Plan: Discovering the Real Meaning of the Life You Planned Before You Were Born*, by Robert Schwartz. It echoes the same idea. Using the intuitive gifts of some talented mediums, the author describes what he calls "pre-birth planning sessions," in which soul groups plan to experience polarizing events so as to raise consciousness through conflict.

"Remember *Your Soul's Plan*, Sharon?" I asked. "The intuitives in that book say families and communities are groups of souls incarnating together time and again. That we take turns embracing one viewpoint after another in each lifetime."

"Yes. Remind me. What did they say is the reason for that?" Sharon asked.

"So that in each lifetime, through our lived experience, we understand every perspective. And over several such births, we learn both differentiation and integration."

"Integration?" Sharon looked puzzled.

"Yes," I went on. "Integration is the awareness of our deep connectedness despite our differences. As Thich Nhat Hanh would say, we are not separate beings but 'inter-are,' sharing a single consciousness."

"Fascinating!" Sharon said. "Every culture uses different approaches, but all aim at building a sense of self that can withstand the storms of life."

We soon came to the end of our walk and said our goodbyes, grateful for the return of spring and another enlightening discussion.

I returned to my day, but the conversation continued in my mind. Triangles had long symbolized energy. Nearly every symbol in the chakra system has one or more triangles. As I did my household chores, I couldn't get over how old the theme of triangulation is yet how current and universal it remains. Stories from many cultures have spoken about the role of the third in conflict.

The well-known Cherokee tale of the two wolves, for example, addresses conflicts in the human psyche. In the story, a grandfather explains to his grandson that there are two wolves fighting within him, a metaphor for the opposing voices inside each of us. After some thinking, the grandson asks, "Which wolf will win?" The old man gives a simple reply: "The one you feed."

Revisiting the story, I now recognized the one choosing which wolf to feed as the third presence in addition to the two wolves. This is the chooser who affects the entire system by their choice, even if the choice is not to choose. Moving away from defining ourselves by the choices we make and their outcomes and moving toward claiming our identity as the chooser is the self-differentiation that Sharon spoke of.

Such a shift is freeing and empowering, and I rewrote the expression "Beggars cannot be choosers" into "Choosers cannot be beggars."

The story of the two wolves reminded me of yet another story, one from Hindu mythology. This one involves the ongoing battle between the gods and the demons for dominion over the heavens. As per this tale, the two sides learn that there is a pot filled with the nectar of immortality, something that would give them freedom from death. Both sides want it badly, but the nectar is at the very depths of the ocean, and only through the churning of the ocean will the nectar rise to the surface.

Realizing they need each other to obtain the nectar, the gods and demons decide to work together. Summoning the greatest mountain on Earth to be their churning rod, they wrap the mythical giant serpent Vasuki around it. With the gods on one side and the demons on the other, they begin to churn the ocean. After initially spitting out poison, the ocean gradually coughs up many treasures, one after another, with the life-preserving nectar finally emerging from its depths.

I had been a conflict-averse person all my life, so these insights made me take a second look at the role of conflict.

With Mother, I had stopped bringing up certain subjects after she iterated her boundary, yet a big part of me was still feeling unsettled, waiting to be seen and affirmed by her. But Sharon had given me a new perspective, suggesting that my real problem was not Mother but an underlying anxiety that made it difficult for me to handle disagreement. This anxiety came from within our family system, was older than our present struggles, and was not personal. The systemic view changed the way I saw my struggles. The discomfort that I was feeling was something I had signed up to feel and release. That was my dharma, or right action, regardless of how Mother chose to show up.

In playing my part, I would be raising myself and, thereby, the entire family system.

I remembered the words in the *Gita*, the setting for which is the battlefield: "Blessed are warriors who are given the chance of a battle like this, which calls them to do what is right and opens the gates of heaven."

Heaven is not up in the skies. It is a realm of infinite possibilities within. As we do our inner work of churning at the depths while keeping our hearts open, our conflicts become sacred gateways to that realm.

CHAPTER REFLECTIONS

1. Think of your family relationships. Who is the black sheep? Can you shift from seeing them as the black sheep to recognizing the underlying family-wide fears they picked up? Send love, compassion, and blessings to them.

2. If you see yourself as having played that role, release the blackness of the shame and guilt, and reflect on Sharon's words: "The family focuses their anxiety on that one person and avoids dealing with their own issues. The black sheep could have the great opportunity to do some deep personal digging and come out healthier on the other end." Explore ways to support yourself in the role your soul has undertaken to play.

CHAPTER 16

GROUNDING IN GROUNDLESSNESS

INSIGHT #14
*By letting go of the impermanent outside,
we connect with the permanent within.*

IT HAD BEEN SIX years since my prophetic conversation with Guruji, and many things had improved vastly over those years. My children were in a better place, finding their strengths and learning to cope with their challenges. The studio was also finding its own niche. More and more people were understanding my approach to well-being as "mental-emotional Yoga" and exploring their inner world through the lens of the spiritual teachings I was sharing.

Although life was not yet all bright and sunny, I was feeling much better every day. Two more years remained of my sade sati, and I believed I had made it through the worst without needing the medication Cathie Dunal, my physician, had suggested. I kept to my daily regimen with various self-care practices, including the snake worship, even as I continued to study and apply the wisdom teachings to my own life.

Of late, I had been reflecting deeply on the teachings of groundlessness, a term that I had heard for the first time in Ani Pema's *The Places That Scare You*. Groundlessness refers to unpredictability, a fundamental fact of life. Happiness from earthly experiences, while not impossible, is impermanent. Possessing anything comes with the risk of losing it. When we face such a loss with an open heart and make room for the accompanying feelings of emptiness, we befriend groundlessness and cultivate true courage. But as human beings, instead of facing the truth, we try to find ways to remain in the illusion and hold on to one thing or another, trading reality for a false sense of security. It is our attachment to victory and safety that ultimately causes us pain.

The idea of surrendering control in the face of groundlessness is an oft-repeated teaching, and I had heard it several times already, from the *Gita* to Elizabeth Lesser to *The Greatness of Saturn*, but I had never seen it modeled for me in my life experiences.

I had encountered people who were attached and controlling, and others who were emotionally detached and unavailable—both strategies to avoid facing defeat. But how does one surrender control without giving up altogether, as the teachings say? How does one stay engaged without attachment? The middle path is not an easy one to take.

Thanks to the Buddhist teachings, for the first time, I was learning that true nonattachment could be cultivated. We can learn, through practice, how to love something deeply and embrace its transience at the same time.

Ani Pema explained this idea in her wise and simple way:

When we resist change, it's called suffering. But when we can completely let go and not struggle against it, when we can embrace the groundlessness of our situation and relax into its dynamic quality, that's called enlightenment.

I revisited my earlier notes to myself. These were my instructions: "Feel it and breathe it. Don't fear it. Don't feed it. Don't fix it. Don't file it. Feel it and free it."

Those cues to open myself to feeling my way through difficult emotions had helped me move away from taking things personally or freezing under their impact. But I sensed there was still some unfinished work there. I needed to go deeper and sink my teeth into the underlying fear of groundlessness.

That was the next step to becoming the third little pig from the story I returned to time and again. I added another line: "Feel it and face it."

It seemed simple enough but was not easy. We are wired to protect ourselves from experiencing groundlessness. Fear, our first responder, offers us various stories and defenses. By attaching to them, we defend ourselves from uncertainty instead of facing it.

I picked up my journal, wanting to list the specific areas of groundlessness and the attachments I had to counter it. As always, I turned to the chakra system to map them out.

CHAKRA	REALM	FEAR	ATTACHMENT TO
One	Physical	Death	Physical Wellness
Two	Emotional	Rejection	Praise and Appreciation
Three	Mental	Uncertainty	Success and Perfection
Four	Relational	Aloneness	Connection
Five	Creative	Irrelevance	Purpose and Work
Six	Intellectual	Blindsiding	Knowledge
Seven	Spiritual	Unknown	Religion

They say a chain is only as strong as its weakest link. I reviewed the list, looking for my weakest link, and found more than one. Rejection and aloneness were the fears that were still raw and needed "cooking." Those were second and fourth chakras. I circled them and made a mental note to remain alert for opportunities to face the groundlessness and, hopefully someday, give up my habit of holding on.

* * *

Ask, and it shall be given! Very soon thereafter came just the opening I was looking for.

Early one morning, as I sipped my usual cup of coffee and just before starting my huddle, I checked my email. A message had come in late at night from Julie, a beloved student who had long supported my work, often sending many others my way. I clicked on her message.

Julie began her email by thanking me for all she had received during the many years she had studied with me. I felt a sinking feeling in my stomach, as this was not the first email that had started this way. I knew what was coming.

Julie had found a new path and a new teacher and would now be going in another direction. She would always remember me with great fondness and respect, she wrote, and wished I would continue to "shine my light" in our community.

A dark cloud descended over what had been a regular morning thus far. I felt the proverbial rug being pulled out from beneath my feet. I had not realized how attached I had grown to this lovely person. Within minutes, I was miserable, feeling lost and rejected even as I was grateful for the opportunity to face this sinking feeling I had run away from all my life.

Students leaving the nest is an integral part of every teacher's experience. Even Ani Pema had written that there are three relationships that truly challenge us and provide great opportunities for growth, and the one between a spiritual teacher and their student is among them. (The other two are the relationship between lovers and the relationship between a parent and child.) While my misery loved the comforting thought that I was not alone in this, I still needed to face my fear of rejection and loss. I drank what remained of my coffee and, after setting the empty cup in the sink, headed to the basement.

Every day, I descended the stairs to meet my huddle and continue my excavations. As I closed my eyes to the outer world that day, I noticed the scared faces of my many selves in the huddle. One was replaying past memories and conversations with Julie and feeling sad that those times were ending. Another felt betrayed after all the affection and effort I had directed Julie's way. A third voice was that of self-doubt, wondering if something was missing in my work and teachings, while a fourth wondered if I was even worthy of being a teacher in the community. In addition, the voices of guilt and shame showed up for experiencing those feelings instead of feeling happy for Julie. They asked, "Why did I have to make it all about myself?"

I stepped back from all of those voices and looked deeper.

Goodbyes had never been easy for me. I had actively tried to avoid them. When family or friends from out of town visited, I was always part of the reception committee, waiting to welcome them at the airport or at our doorstep. When it came time to say goodbye, however, I would make excuses and busy myself. The finality of farewells and the one-way movement of time was just not something I had the capacity to digest.

Even my high school English teacher, Mrs. Dhall, had noticed my difficulty with partings. In those days, we requested a personal farewell note in our autograph books before graduating and leaving for college. When she reached for my book and began to write, she said, "I know just the words I want to leave you with."

She wrote a beautiful verse inspiring me to trust goodbyes, let go, and move on. But even though I remembered her message, it had not sunk in.

On the contrary, I had created a bunch of tricks for holding on and escaping goodbyes—people pleasing, avoiding conflicts, and working hard to maintain friendships and connections. There was love, of course—a lot of it—but fear of loss had contaminated that love. Like a person falling off a mountain, I would hold on to one frail tree after another, hoping to be saved.

No more. I believe we all come to Earth with some big projects to work on, and this was certainly one of mine. Looking around at the scared faces in my huddle, I declared it was time to let go, hit the ground, and see what I might find there. I was going to teach myself to gracefully open the door even wider to someone who wanted to leave, acknowledging feelings of longing, sadness, and nostalgia but without validating them as I used to. I was so attached to my past that I wanted it to continue forever!

Suddenly I thought of Mother, who spent her mental energy scheduling actions and planning future events. Although our approach was different, we were both trying to escape the uncertainty of the present. I was invested in the past, and she in the future.

What lies beneath all this uncertainty? I wondered. *What am I running away from? What am I avoiding?*

I kept asking the question, going deeper and deeper within, looking for answers. I was going to use Julie's departure to finally confront the wolf in its own den.

Uncovering the stories I was scaring myself with, I saw images of this student leaving and sparking an exodus of others. My fearful imagination was exaggerating the situation.

So what?

More fearful images. Many others leaving.

So what?

There would be no need for my teachings or me.

So what?

Nobody needs me. I am alone and—

Feel it, don't think it.

I felt as if the ground beneath me were opening up. I was entering groundlessness.

Keep going. Keep falling.

I let go of any attempts to hold on. I was hurtling down a black hole.

Let it go, let it go, drop the resistance.

I was in a deep, dark place, drowning in doom.

Let go, go deeper, breathe.

I let myself drown and embraced the darkness, no longer fighting it.

Silence.

The darkness and I were one.

More silence. Stillness.

Staying with the groundlessness, releasing the waves of fear, one breath at a time.

A long silence. With deepening darkness.

The sound of voices.

I see us, our family of four. We are in the darkness of Mammoth Caves. I recognize the long-forgotten memory coming up. Miles and miles of caves in sheer darkness, with not a drop of light coming in.

Our guide is speaking. His flashlight is directed at the blind crayfish swimming in a pond in a corner of the cave.

"They don't need sight as we know it," he explains. "*Over years of evolution, nature has replaced their sense of sight with other intelligence. They are now thriving differently, as this environment demands. Life always finds a way, even in the darkness. Life always finds a way.*"

The words echoed in my mind, returning my awareness to the present. I opened my eyes and looked around, realizing I was still at home, in my basement. An hour had passed since I began the morning's huddle.

The memory that had surfaced was from many years earlier, a moment I had forgotten.

We were still relatively new in the US then, maybe two or three years in, when we visited the Mammoth Caves, the world's longest known cave system. Over the weekend, we had seen several parts of it. This particular scene was noteworthy, with its profound message: "Life always finds a way."

The blind crayfish, in the darkest of places of the world, had survived and were thriving. Not because of any one person, not because of any rescue, but because the hand of nature protects and preserves in places and ways the human mind cannot fathom.

In the darkest of places within myself, I had found the light of hope.

God, Mother Nature, Universe, Mystery, Source. One Creator—many names. And now, life. Seeing God as life took these concepts to a deeper and far more pervasive level than I had ever imagined. Life—a presence that contains within it all aspects of living and dying, and all stages of evolution for all life-forms, including me. Life continuing through the various twists and turns as we transform from one state to another.

I had always imagined groundlessness as falling into a bottomless pit. Similarly, I imagined grounding meant finding something solid, stable, and unchanging. But my experience changed my understanding. With no solid ground beneath me, groundlessness felt like falling into a safety net.

I remembered seeing a safety net at the circus as a child. My family would go every year as a special event. Dad would stand in line weeks beforehand to buy tickets, and the whole family looked forward to it with excitement. The trapeze act was one of my favorites. We watched, holding our breath as they swung to great heights and performed all kinds of acrobatics. Every once in a while, a trapeze artist would fall, and everyone would exclaim in fear. Down and down they would go, into the safety net. After bouncing to a stop, they would get back on their feet and continue their airborne movements.

We are like those trapeze artists as we swing through the opposites of pleasure and pain. Every now and then, we are tossed off course. To be grounded is not about holding on to permanence through possessions, achievements, and relationships. It is a firm inner knowing that we are supported by life even as we are falling. People and fortunes come and go. Our connection to something more abiding sustains us—an intelligence that both permeates and transcends the opposites of high and low.

Practicing groundlessness asks us to sink our roots deeper, beyond the fear-driven instinct to control uncontrollable situations of our lives. Trusting the invisible safety net is our best choice in the face of impermanence. When we are falling, we can let go, knowing we will be held, and start over.

I began reflecting on the difficult times in my life. Picking up my journal, I started what I called The Silver Lining Exercise. Listing each dark period, I thought about who or what had gotten me through that time. Sometimes a friend or a neighbor, often an inspiring book, once even a line from a soap opera! In hindsight, I recognized that life had not always been perfect. But it had, indeed, managed to find a way to continue—every time.

Only a couple of hours had passed since I started my reflections, but I felt like a new person. I was ready to respond to Julie. In the past, this would have been an excruciating feat, but I felt calm now. I replied to her, expressing my gratitude for our time together, my sadness over the empty space she left behind, and my understanding of her need to move on. I sent her blessings on her new journey, assuring her of my ongoing support. When I hit Send, I felt sad and light at the same time. Life would hold me as old doors closed and new ones opened.

I felt a sense of victory over my victimhood with goodbyes. There would be more, of course, but each time, I would face the emptiness of partings without shrinking. Freedom from attachment does not happen without practice—over and over again. We need to choose letting go, trusting the ground of groundlessness.

I looked through my big box of mementos and pulled out my autograph book. It was time to revisit Mrs. Dhall's verse about farewells:

Think that life is a stairway, on which you must climb to the skies,
And strive that the climbing be higher as each one away from you flies.

How wise were her words, reminding me to uplift myself even as others took flight! I was filled with gratitude for my former teacher's timeless advice and sent a silent thank-you her way, wherever she might be.

Our journeys are eternal, even if the ones we travel with and the paths we follow are not.

We continue.

CHAPTER REFLECTIONS

1. Look over the chakra list to discover your areas of fear.

2. Have you experienced those fears and losses before? How did you pull yourself through that time? Who or what was the silver lining during those times? How did that happen? Reflect on the hand of Life/Universe/God/Source that sends us people to support us even when things don't unfold the way we wish.

3. Trusting the journey is ultimately a stand we take. Can you take the stand to trust life unconditionally and lean into your fears a little every day? If not, what holds you back?

CHAPTER 17

A NEW OLD RELATIONSHIP

INSIGHT #15

*Our primary relationship is with life itself and forms
the foundation for all other relationships.*

THE MAMMOTH CAVES MEMORY replayed itself in my mind, reminding me of the words of Joseph Campbell, the renowned thinker and teacher of comparative mythology: "The cave you fear to enter holds the treasure you seek." I was intrigued by how significant these words were in my own journey. I was still not sure whether the memory had been a mystical experience or just an old recollection popping up, but I did find a gift—a priceless insight for living with uncertainty.

The tour guide's words, "Life always finds a way," coupled with the image of the blind crayfish thriving in the darkness, continued to make inroads in my relationship with God. Life was opening a door and inviting me to a new relationship with reality—a relationship built on trusting, not fearing, the unknown, and working with it, just as the crayfish had done to survive and thrive in complete darkness. As I journaled about these new possibilities, I remembered another time in my life when I'd had a similar breakthrough that renewed my connection to Source. It was nearly nineteen years earlier, when Krish had been assigned a project in Tel Aviv, Israel. Since the undertaking was expected to last several months, our family relocated. We had one child then, our son, Anish, who was a few months shy of turning four.

Once we had settled into our beautiful sea-facing apartment, Krish threw himself into his work, and I found a day care for our firstborn. Over time, I established my routine: reading, taking walks by the beach, visiting museums, watching television, and making trips to Jerusalem, which was about forty-five minutes away.

After a few guided tours, I became familiar with the old city and was comfortable roaming around on my own. Jerusalem soon became my favorite place in the world. I loved the ancient structures and the intriguing scenes of past and present living within each other. Having not learned much about the history of that side of the world during my formal education, I was reading a lot to catch up.

Jerusalem is the center of three principal faiths of the Western world. Raised in India, where religion and spirituality are central to daily life, I watched, fascinated, as groups of tourists and pilgrims arrived, listening to their guides in languages foreign to me. Hinduism as a religion is extremely broadminded and recognizes all faiths as different paths toward the same God. While this openness allowed me to enjoy studying other faiths, I still had my identity firmly planted in Hinduism.

On the afternoon of my breakthrough, I sat on the steps to the courtyard in front of the Church of the Holy Sepulchre. The church was built where Christ's execution and burial took place and is also known as the Church of the Crucifixion. Right inside was the Stone of Anointing, a slab of rock believed to be where Christ's body was prepared for burial. From where I sat,

I had a direct view of this stone. Some people were sitting on the floor with their hands upon it, praying.

I watched them, devout Christians, with my Hindu eyes, respecting their faith but fenced into my own. One woman had her eyes closed as tears were streaming down; she seemed to be battling something painful. The sight of her tears touched me, and I could not look away, compelled by a need to see what would happen next.

As I continued to watch, her expression slowly changed. Something shifted inside her, and a gentle smile appeared. She had found peace. Within.

Her transformation struck me deeply. Here she was, this weary traveler who had come from miles away, seeking God, only to sit here and find the object of her search within. It is the way of the pilgrim—to journey far and wide, only to find what one is looking for so close to home. Religions, no matter their differences, arrive at the same place. And that place is within—never separated from us.

Faith is a universal human experience, just like joy, humor, and love. Just like humor is universal while jokes are circumstantial, faith is universal, but religion is regional. It is said that a translated joke dies. Only when it's told in a certain context does it entertain. Religion is the same; it needs to be experienced in its own cultural and geographic context to connect us to the faith within.

* * *

In the wake of that insight, my visits to the various churches and mosques, and to the Wailing Wall, changed as I meditated and prayed in each place. In ways I had not expected, opening my heart to other religions fed my own faith.

Mahatma Gandhi, in response to someone who asked him if he was Hindu, had replied, "Yes, I am. I am also a Muslim, a Christian, a Buddhist, and a Jew."

I felt the same. Like people, religions are not perfect. But every religion, with its unique focus, brings a piece of the puzzle to the bigger mystery of our Creator. If we can learn different languages and take pride in doing so, why can't we also embrace different religions and take joy in them? I shifted from respectfully tolerating other religions with unconscious superiority to embracing them as another way of finding the divine within—and everywhere else.

Looking back on that memory, I realized that despite the big shift of seeing the divine as inherent within every being, I still believed we had to earn access to that presence. The God I believed in favored good over evil, perfection over imperfection, light over darkness. Many believers talk about God as "light." Spiritual awakening is "en-light-enment." People "shine their light" on Earth.

We tend to compartmentalize light and darkness and see them as two separate realities. Light means all good things—health, virtue, success, and so on. People enjoying these gifts are said to be blessed. On the other hand, suffering—illness, distress, and failure—is connected with darkness. Are people going through adversities not blessed? Are they being punished? Has God turned away from them?

With my breakthrough of finding divine presence within the darkness, a new perspective was emerging. God is an infinitely intelligent life force whose presence keeps us company and carries us through the dark nights of life. It is human beings who are wired to pursue pleasure over pain. The Bible says that God created man in his own image. We, in turn, had done the same, humanizing God and interpreting pleasure and joy as signs of God's presence and approval and seeing pain and discomfort as indications of God's rejection and admonishment. But God is not a fair-weather friend who abandons you when things go wrong.

I was reminded of a scene from a holiday our family had taken in India a few years earlier. We were touring a coffee estate in a jeep with Sujay, the owner of the property, when a sudden cloudburst surprised us. The rain came down sharp and heavy, and the wheels of our vehicle were soon entrenched in mud. Despite his attempts, Sujay could not get the wheels to budge. He tried again and again, but we were getting nowhere.

A while later, a man from the neighborhood drove past. Lowering his window, he hollered to Sujay, "Stop turning those wheels! You are digging your vehicle deeper. Just sit tight for now. I am headed to town and will send you help."

Some thirty minutes later, a truck arrived with the equipment needed to rescue the jeep. The mud was slick and did not want to let go, but our vehicle was slowly eked out, and we got back on the road.

This, I now believed, was what God is like—the unbiased force capable of pulling us out of inextricable situations when we relentlessly spin the wheels of our human effort, only to dig ourselves deeper into our mess. The emotional pain we attribute to our problems is really a longing for a more personal, more meaningful connection with something bigger.

The word *religion* has its roots in the Latin *religare*, meaning "to bind," just as the word *Yoga* has its roots in the Sanskrit *yuj*, meaning "to yoke." Both *religion* and *Yoga* are meant to unite us with the Creator, who can pull us out of our stuck places. But concepts of sin and karma, coming from an interpretation of God as only light, not darkness, have left us divided from within.

Looking at that split in myself, I revisited the conversations I had with Sharon about emotional triangles. She said that stress between two people causes triangulation with a third in order to stabilize the system. We had spoken about this in the context of the conflicts in external relationships, but I was now applying the concept to the inner world as well. The two principal voices in the inner world are those of the inner child (the natural self) and the inner adult (the ego self that is managing interactions in the outer environment). The inner child is who we are, and the ego is who we believe we should be. This creates stress and requires a third to bring about balance.

Who is the third for me? I wondered, looking within. There was my inner child, the little girl in red, my very soul, a drop of the divine who, like her Creator, was both perfect and imperfect. On the other end stood my adult self, facing the world outside and trying to meet expectations.

And then I recognized my third. It was my inner critic. She was powerful. Like the conductor of an orchestra, she set the vision for my huddle—a vision of perfection and control. A goal that was basically unattainable.

I had believed that voice to be a spokesperson of God and allowed myself to be driven by it. But that was not God at all. Rather, it was the echo of a polarized culture. It had worked for a long time. But faced with adversity, my adult self, like Sujay's vehicle, had been stuck. Caught between my imperfect inner child and the perfectionist controller masquerading as God, I could really go nowhere.

This felt like a huge insight.

The third voice in my psyche, my inner critic, needed to be retired. Given that we humans are imperfect and adversity is unavoidable, the third in our inner triangle needs to be a voice that can support us unconditionally and help us work with what is.

The *Gita* describes God as an equanimous, loving presence that is beyond the opposites of right and wrong. I was going to change my inner world with that unconditional presence becoming the third in the tango between my inner child and my inner adult. Faith and courage, not fear, would be the guiding force within.

My spiritual practices now had a new purpose. All my prayers, Yoga, and breathwork were no longer activities to please a controlling God or a way to make up for past transgressions. Instead, they were ways to connect to that unconditional loving presence within—the third in the internal triangle that would bring equilibrium and stability to the system.

* * *

Pranayama is the Yogic practice of breathwork, which I studied as part of my training in Kundalini Yoga. But as I approached it with my new intention and understanding, I was starting to see breath as an unbiased, animating energy with consciousness. Over the years of my emotional struggles, I made it a point to breathe as I confronted difficult situations. But now I asked myself, *Why is breath so magically calming? Who gives us our breath? What makes all creatures breathe, whether on land, in the skies, or underwater? How do plants know to breathe?*

Scientists can explain respiration as an interchange between oxygen and carbon dioxide. Their focus is on the role of breath in the dance between the sympathetic and parasympathetic nervous systems. In pranayama practice, the focus is on counting the inhales and exhales, holding the breath, and so on.

Science and Yoga are two different disciplines, but both see breath as something that, when managed and modulated, brings benefits beyond the physical. But for me, breath is awareness. My breath is as aware of me as I am of it. In Latin, the word for breath is *spiritus*. Spirit. The ancients knew this.

Life force is prana shakti in Sanskrit. Prana shakti is spirit. It comes to Earth with our first breath and leaves with us when we take our last. Between the first breath and the last, life remains hidden in the background, silently staying the course. On good days and bad, whether friends stay or leave, the one steady companion that holds us, unconditionally available to us, is our breath. Breath gives us life. Breath is life. And breath has life.

My reflections anchored me deeper in my breath. I marveled at how the act of breathing is both a universal and a personal connection to Source. Billions of life-forms on Earth are breathing simultaneously, yet we each enjoy our own breath. Often, as I worked, walked, or read, I would simply pause and turn my attention to my breath, much like a child at play looks to its mother to make sure she is still around. On good days, I loved the simple act of touching base with life. On days when I did not believe in myself, I was reassured by the thought that life still believed in me enough to give me a new breath, a new chance.

The shift in me was palpable. All those years, I had believed in a God I did not really trust. Belief in God is intellectual. Loving God is emotional. But trusting God is visceral. Faith, when embodied, becomes trust.

I sensed the healing of an old wound. Not a physical or even an emotional one, but a spiritual wound—the quiet ache of divine rejection and abandonment from earlier lifetimes.

With each passing day, I sensed my connection to this fountainhead of life growing deeper and stronger. And the connection I was making within was shifting how I showed up in the world. I was less needy, more content and confident, and able to love people in a whole new way that felt more genuine.

A realization was beginning to dawn: Our primary relationship is with life—this mysterious something that births everything, sustains everything, and to which we all return. Some people might call that God. Humans have fought battles over naming, owning, and expressing it. I simply called it life, and through healing this intangible relationship, all other relationships were becoming healthier.

The *Gita* declares, "As a man's faith is, so is he."

My faith had experienced an upgrade, and with that, my own freedom had begun. Faith was the building material I needed to build that stable home for the third little pig I was becoming.

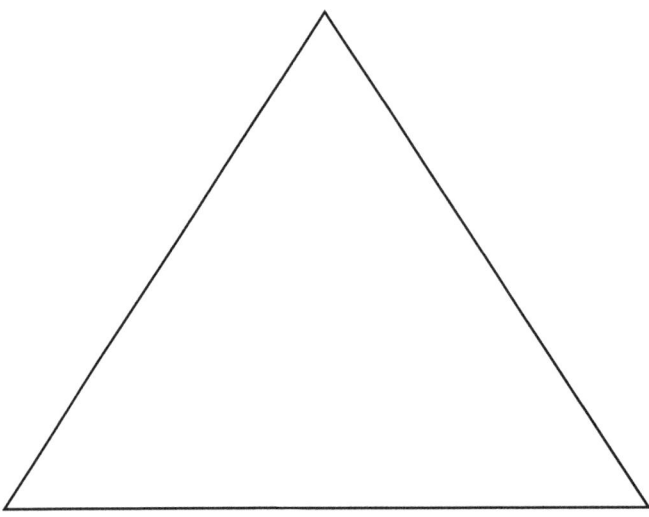

The Third

~~A Perfectionist, Punishing, Critical God~~
A Compassionate, Supportive, and Integrative Being

Inner Child

Emotional
Intuitive
Raw

Inner Adult

Rational
Factual
Goal-Oriented

The Inner Triangle

CHAPTER REFLECTIONS

1. Our relationship with our breath is the oldest and most lasting one we will have on this Earth. Reflect on the magical act of respiration that we were all born knowing how to do. As you breathe, connect to all of creation, which you, too, are a part of.

2. Pause as often as you can during your day to take mindful breaths, seeing each breath as an embrace with life, the mystery that gives each of us our daily breaths.

CHAPTER 18

A PAUSE FOR CELEBRATION

INSIGHT #16
Good friends are companions needed for the journey.

IT WAS TIME FOR another birthday celebration, but this time, my friends and I were also celebrating the end of my sade sati, the seven-and-a-half-year period of Saturn. While some of life's problems remained unsolved, things were certainly much better than when I'd started my journey, both at home and at work. Meanwhile, Mother was still keeping up her valiant battle with cancer. The more I accepted her as she was, the more I appreciated her spirit.

My sangha—which Ani Pema described as a place where you can "take off your armor" to be your natural, vulnerable self—had grown over the years, and this core group of eight women had been with me through it all. We had studied the book *The Greatness of Saturn* together and applied its teachings to the many challenges of our lives. As my sade sati drew to a close, my friends were almost as relieved as I was that this difficult period might be ending, at least by astrological indications.

The group decided to make a big deal of the occasion. Robin had a second home in Wisconsin and offered it as the venue for our day-long retreat. As we drove there together, I looked around at my friends' bright and beloved faces and realized how much each of them had contributed to my work and the success of my studio, which was now a busy place.

Robin had provided a boost by starting a store in the studio to sell books, crystals, Yoga mats, and other items to help students on their spiritual journeys. Ann was a gifted intuitive who brought people to the studio with her Tarot card readings. Veronique—or Vero, as we fondly called her—had taken my Reiki lessons to a whole new level and now was leading the Reiki wing of the studio herself. Katie had helped me adapt the teachings of mindfulness to youth and children and was trying to get us into the local schools. Gail, the pragmatic one in the group, helped me with financial planning and negotiating with my landlord over rent—conversations that made me quite uncomfortable! Peggy and Bridget supported me with their encouraging presence, recommending my work to friends and bringing others with them to the studio. Sharon, of course, was my go-to person, who remained generously available to me with her input and advice as a friend and a psychotherapist herself. She was also the person who helped me stay the course every time I felt unworthy and ready to give up the studio.

My little sangha had brought food, refreshments, and great plans to celebrate our love and sisterhood. We had an amazing lunch, after which we sat in chairs, drinking tea in the backyard. It was a beautiful fall afternoon, and the sun was shining on the turning leaves, with orange and yellow reflecting the light. Robin's cottage faced a little lake, whose serene waters mirrored the trees' beauty.

Gail spoke first. "So, Ramaa, now that your seven-and-a-half has ended, can you summarize your experience for us? How did it go, and how are you feeling now?"

"Great question, Gail. Yes, go ahead. Tell us," encouraged Vero.

I gave the waiting faces a long look. Bittersweet thoughts and memories of the past years flashed through my mind as I turned to the quiet lake, collecting my thoughts.

"Let me start at the very beginning. As you all know, I had been teaching from my home and wanting to expand my reach. I moved to a studio space, ready to take on the world! Unfortunately for me, it was around then that I entered my sade sati and began the first of its three parts, although I did not know it then. I liken that time to the first stage of consciousness that the *Gita* talks about—blissful ignorance."

"The first little pig!" Katie added, remembering my favorite analogy.

"Yes!" I smiled at her as I went on. "In this first part, many problems cropped up. My studio did not quite take off as I had imagined. At home, unexpected situations arose. As the first little pig, I ran here and there, my bubble of ignorance popped, as I tried many things but did not really find a solution."

"I remember that stage well," said Sharon, my sounding board for years.

"Then came the second stage of this journey," I continued. "I became increasingly emotional, and Mother said she could not deal with me anymore. Usha had things going on in her own life. I was on my own. At first, I felt abandoned, but I was morphing into the second little pig. Teachers seemed to emerge from out of nowhere. I was learning a lot about myself, my family, and our souls' journeys together."

"Was it during this time that you did your certification program with the Jung Institute?" Robin asked.

"Yes, that two-year program fell right within this period. As did my learning with Anodea Judith about the psychology of the chakras, finding the teachings of Buddhism, and so much more. The Universe was very generous in sending me help."

I paused, feeling overwhelmed as I remembered the many synchronistic events of those times. My eyes welled up with tears of gratitude. Somebody passed me tissues as they all waited patiently.

I started again. "Always being a good student, this time, also, I learned my lessons well. Then it was time to grow into the third little pig. This was the hardest part. As the third little pig, I had to go deeper and face the issues at a foundational level."

"Sounds like root chakra work," said Ann.

"It is indeed," I said. "At the very root of all problems is our own fear of groundlessness. And that is ultimately the wolf we each have to face from time to time. The third little pig is not a permanent title but a position one takes—a choice in the moment. Letting go and trusting the unknown was excruciating and challenging. But just when I thought I was falling into a deep, dark hole, I realized there is light in darkness and darkness in light. This was a big realization, and it released me from many beliefs I had been stuck in since childhood. It opened up a new way of relating to life—more openness, less fear. And, of course, as I learned new things, I upgraded my teaching curriculum to pass it on to our community."

I finished my summary of seven and a half years, realizing for the first time just how much had transpired.

"We love the way you reinvent the teachings again and again," Bridget offered kindly.

"I think that teaching in your unique way is you finding your voice, like King V did in the story," added Sharon, using the shortened version of Vikramaditya's name that the group had settled on.

I reflected on Sharon's point. "You're right, Sharon. Years ago, when Guruji initiated me into Kundalini Yoga, he said that someday I would have

We were nearly done when Sharon spoke. "Want to share your wish with us, Rumster?"

"Sure. Would love to." I put my plate down and wiped the crumbs off my mouth. "But first, do you remember the last part of King Vikramaditya's story?"

"Help us, please. It's been a few years," Ann said, laughing.

"It is at the end of the seven-and-a-half, when Saturn asks the king to make a wish," I explained. "Vikramaditya requests Saturn to spare others from the pain he experienced. I was thinking of that as I made my wish. May my family, my community, and my world be spared the growing pains I went through."

"That's beautiful," said Sharon.

"Thank you. While success helps us feel special, it can harden the ego, creating walls of separateness. Struggles thaw us so we can flow down from that isolating mountaintop to connect with others like us and uplift one another."

"I like the idea of our suffering bringing connection and relief to our world," Peggy said. Then she suggested that we all meditate on the theme together.

"Are you ladies up for a meditation?" I asked.

There was a heartfelt "Yes!" as we all sat up and prepared to meditate. I led the group, recalling the Buddhist teachings on tonglen, the practice of giving and receiving blessings. As we closed our eyes and opened our hearts, I invited each of my friends to dig deep into what was hurting them the most. Then, instead of feeling sad and isolated in our pain, we let it open our hearts to all those in the world suffering like us. And we sent blessings of well-being to ourselves and our world.

A fitting tribute to Saturn and his mission on the earthly realm.

*　*　*

to find my own ways to teach the practice. That is what I have started [to do]. And I owe you all a big thanks for staying the course with me. Your su[pport] has helped me clarify my thinking and share the message with so [many] others."

Once again, my heart overflowed with gratitude, and my eyes filled [with] tears. This time, we were all weeping. These past years had brought chall[enges] for each of us, but we had been there for each other as unconditional p[illars] of support.

The tears done, we sat quietly for a few minutes.

It was Robin who spoke next. "So, how are you feeling now, Ramaa[, and] where do you go from here?"

It didn't take me long to know my answer. "I am feeling like an en[tirely] different person from who I was seven and a half years ago. Then, I was u[pbeat] and positive on the outside but quite scared deep down. I can see that cl[early] now, and I am grateful to Saturn for breaking me open. These years have [been] painful, of course, but with that pain, I have grown and learned to trus[t in a] way I never did before. Even my relationships have changed and become [more] honest and peaceful."

I paused and sighed before continuing. "Having said all that, I don't t[hink] Saturn is done with me yet, sade sati or not. I sense there are more les[sons] coming my way, and I pray that I stay awake and move forward without fa[lling] back into old patterns."

Again, we sat quietly. Robin and Vero exchanged a look and suddenly w[ent] into the house, reemerging with a cake topped with a candle.

"Aw, you shouldn't have," I said as they placed it on the center table. [The] cake read, "Hooray to the end of the 7 1/2!"

"Make a wish!" they ordered.

I did, and I blew out the candle. Then we focused on the important w[ork] of tucking into the delicious slices of cake.

A PAUSE FOR CELEBRATION

Life continued upward in the following months. While there were no dramatic events, the quality of my life was definitely changing, and there were fewer mornings of waking up with a heavy dread. I mostly woke up with an insight, a flash of inspiration, or a word or image, as if someone had left me a secret message to decode. I still followed my huddle routine, but instead of unpacking my morning blues, I was unpacking my morning clues! Sometimes, they would lead to deep insights. Other times, they would begin an entirely new journey.

One morning, I woke up to memories of our family's stay in Israel. Many different images were flashing across my mind, and a great longing to return arose in my heart. I also thought of my dear Israeli friend, Simi, whom I knew from our stay there. She was a warm, beautiful person, and we had stayed in touch over the years.

In the week that followed, the Holy Land kept coming up in conversation in the most unexpected places. I wondered if I was being called to visit. After thinking about it for some time, I sent Simi a message that simply read, "I am missing your country and wish I could return." Having sent the message, I retired for the night, leaving my yearnings in the hands of the Universe.

CHAPTER REFLECTIONS

1. **Tonglen is the Buddhist practice of giving and receiving. We breathe in the darkness of the world and breathe out the light of our divinity as blessings to the world. This was the meditation I did with my friends. Practice this meditation. Start by sitting in a quiet place and calming yourself. Then think of something that is worrying you, and soften your heart by reminding yourself that you are not alone. Thousands of people on the planet are suffering just like you. On the inhale, breathe in your pain and darkness. On the exhale, send blessings and good wishes to yourself and others suffering like you. This is how we transform our internal pain into blessings for ourselves and others.**

The Saturn Sisters at a birthday celebration

PART 5

ONE-ING

CHAPTER 19

UPLIFTING DOWNFALLS IN THE HOLY LAND

INSIGHT #17
All faith traditions see God as the integration of the opposites.

I WOKE UP TO JOYFUL and excited responses from Simi. She worked for a travel company and was eager to know what arrangements I needed from her. I was touched to see how welcoming and generous she was in opening up her home and her schedule for my stay.

When I first met Simi nineteen years earlier, she was single. She had visited us in our home in Chicago once, but that was seventeen years before, when we were still new to the city ourselves. Now she was married, a mother to three, and living in a kibbutz on the outskirts of Tel Aviv.

I planned my trip thoughtfully. I wanted to stay in Tel Aviv and visit my favorite streets and markets for old times' sake before traveling farther. For the second part of my stay, Simi had made reservations at a hotel right inside the Old City of Jerusalem, which would be an entirely new experience for me. I started making my wish list of places to visit and looked forward to my week away.

* * *

On my fourth day in Israel, Simi drove me out of Tel Aviv to old Jerusalem. We had one of those friendships in which you can pick up where you left off, even years later. As we walked through the Old City toward our hotel, my excitement increased upon seeing that we were steps away from the Wailing Wall. I would be staying so close to where generations of history had unfolded. What good fortune to have a friend in the travel industry who knew exactly what I would enjoy!

After spending the day together, Simi returned to her family while I enjoyed walking down familiar cobblestone pathways alone, stopping at shops and ancient sites.

Soon, I was back on the front steps of the Church of the Holy Sepulchre. The connection I had made years earlier felt vividly close and vibrant. I lingered in its newfound depths, recalling that faith is a universal calling and religion is simply the language that expresses it.

Sitting there now, it felt like a homecoming. I watched as a new busload of tourists walked through the church and prayed. Everything seemed the same, yet so much had changed. I reflected on the history of events, both personal and global, since the last time I had sat on those steps.

How little we know about what the future holds, the people we will meet, and the places we will visit. Time slowed down as I gathered up the nineteen years of my life between those two moments on the steps, acknowledging the gains and making peace with the losses. I treasured this opportunity and lingered deliberately, knowing that these few days would go by soon and life would return to its usual pace.

Sitting on a chair facing the Wailing Wall, I enjoyed the gentle sounds of people praying around me. I recalled the words from the *Gita* that describe God as our oldest ancestor and felt comforted by our interrelatedness. I quickly slipped into a meditative state, feeling even more open and relaxed than the last time I had been there.

Later that day, I tried to visit the famous Al-Aqsa Mosque, which is situated right by the Wailing Wall. But times had changed, and tensions between Israel and its neighbors had increased. Non-Muslims were no longer allowed entry. This saddened me, but I had to accept that the entire world had changed after 9/11.

Simi returned to Jerusalem the next day to show me around. We visited places of local interest and toured new excavations. Later that night, we sat in our hotel room, planning the rest of my stay. We were going over my wish list when she received a call from a friend. As Simi spoke, she threw worried glances my way. They were speaking in Hebrew, and I caught the word *Tabgha* coming up often. When Simi hung up, she hastily reached for the remote.

The television was broadcasting the news. A church had been attacked and portions set on fire. This was the famous church of fish and loaves, located in the village of Tabgha, where Christ had miraculously fed thousands with just a bit of fish and bread. Needing that abundance in my own life, I had put the church at the top of my list, hoping to take home some of that energy. But now it would be closed to visitors.

My face fell as I watched the coverage of how much damage the fire had caused. Simi translated the news and tried to cheer me up.

"It's okay," she said. "This means we will spend more time at the other places on your list."

I still felt crushed. Simi tried again. "Look at it as a sign that you must come back to our country for another visit."

It was getting late, and we had been on our feet all day. We were both very tired. Calling it a night, we climbed into our beds and turned off the lights. Shortly thereafter, Simi's quiet breathing told me she was fast asleep.

But I lay in bed awake, wondering about the church fire. *Was it mere coincidence that the church at the top of my list was destroyed the evening before our visit? What are the chances of such timing? Why am I being denied my wish to visit that church? Am I being punished for something I did?*

Try as I might, I could not keep myself from making the event personal. Familiar old sensations of deep unworthiness arose as my mind listed my every imperfection to justify my feelings of divine rejection.

But my thoughts did not completely draw me into their darkness. Ani Pema's words came to mind. She had referred to the human tendency of interpreting "pain as punishment and pleasure as a reward." That was exactly what I was doing. After wrestling with my emotions for a little while more, I dragged myself to practice the Yoga of self-love, saying to myself, *Feel the disappointment. Don't flee it, don't fear it, don't feed it. Let it flow, let it go. Feel it and free it.*

After a few minutes of mindful breathing, I calmed down and "re-minded" myself to take the position of the third little pig, combining disappointment with trust. I still did not know why the church had been damaged on the eve of my visit, but I was open to whatever the morrow might bring. Then I dropped off to sleep.

We were back on the road the next morning, my heart heavy as I said my goodbyes to Jerusalem, wondering if and when I'd ever return to this cherished site again. We drove north to the region around the Sea of Galilee, stopping by Capernaum along the way, the town where Jesus began his ministry. It was in the synagogue in Capernaum that Jesus led his congregation, giving many sermons and performing miracles. I walked through what remained of the place as I imagined what it must have been like. Closing my eyes, I took deep breaths. I wanted to bottle up the energy of this place and take it back home to my own sangha.

Next, we headed to the Church of the Beatitudes, where Christ delivered his Sermon on the Mount. I had felt a special connection to this place the first time we visited years earlier, and I was ready to reconnect with its vibrations.

As she drove us, Simi was curious about my enthusiasm. She asked, "What makes you so interested in these places?"

I smiled, thinking about the many temples of India I always enjoyed visiting. "I don't know. I've always had a special connection to prayer, even as a child. It was my favorite hobby! I connect deeply with spiritual places."

India is a very spiritual country, and we turn to God for everything. I had missed our temples when we first left the country, but over time, the walls in my mind that separated religions had dissolved.

"Now I am happy to pray anywhere I go," I added. "I guess I am an incurable pilgrim!" I turned to face Simi. "What about your connection to these places?" I asked.

Her eyes fixed on the road ahead, Simi sighed and took a long moment to reply.

"So many of the problems in our country stem from religion, which makes me unsure of its role in human life. I have my connection with God, of course. But religion? No, thank you! As a person who organizes travel for others, I draw satisfaction in helping people find what they are looking for, but I have no interest beyond that."

We were quiet for a bit as I reflected on her words. So much that fed me was not a staple diet for my dear friend. Yet each day we had been together, I had watched her. She was more beautiful, more loving, and more generous than many religious people I had known. I saw no reason to change her mind.

When we arrived at the church, Simi dropped me off at the entrance, saying she had a few calls to make and that she would come back for me later.

I wandered around the outside of the church, reading the words of the beatitudes displayed on little boards on the lawn:

> Blessed are the poor in spirit,
> for theirs is the kingdom of heaven.
>
> Blessed are they who mourn, for they will be comforted.
>
> Blessed are the meek, for they will inherit the land.
>
> Blessed are they who hunger and thirst for
> righteousness, for they will be satisfied.
>
> Blessed are the merciful, for they will be shown mercy.
>
> Blessed are the clean of heart, for they will see God.
>
> Blessed are the peacemakers, for they
> will be called children of God.
>
> Blessed are they who are persecuted for the sake of
> righteousness, for theirs is the kingdom of heaven.

There were eight of them. I was reminded of another eight: the eight-fold path of Buddhism that I had delved into in the years since I had last been in this church. That realization felt like an affirmation of the universality of the message.

I entered the church. The inside was circular, a detail I had not remembered. Unlike the temples and churches I had visited before, with the pulpit or altar on one side, here, the altar stood in the center at a great height. Wherever one sat, the altar would be just as near to or far from them as it was for others.

No hierarchy in our humanity, I thought. We are all equidistant from the divine, no matter where we are positioned. And we all need to raise our eyes to a higher consciousness.

The beatitudes were displayed inside the church as well. Choosing a chair close to the entrance, I sat down and closed my eyes, reflecting on their words. All of them basically said that those who faced struggles and stood on the side of righteousness would find something richer and more enduring. I interpreted "kingdom of heaven" as a place with infinite possibilities and understood the beatitudes to mean that those facing earthly poverty would be compelled to look deeper and find the treasure house within.

The message resonated deeply with me. The difficult years of Saturn had presented me with challenging situations and taken many things and people away from me. But thanks to the Yoga of self-love, I had healed and released the pain in my heart. And Nature, abhorring a vacuum, had filled the empty spaces with love and peace. After all these years, and in a much healthier place, I looked back and felt blessed, awash with gratitude for the journey and everyone who had contributed to it—Grandmother, Mother, my family, my sangha, and simply every person who had influenced my path, directly or indirectly.

My visit to the church at Tabgha had been thwarted for a reason. I had been seeking abundance on the outside while still carrying traces of victimhood and inner poverty. But the beatitudes had shed light on the richness within and left me full of gratitude. Now, the events of the past twenty-four hours seemed like the miracle I had really needed.

I opened my eyes and looked around, my gaze settling on the cross above. I noticed the intersection of its two beams—horizontal and vertical. Many religious traditions have intersecting opposites in their symbols. There is the cross, of course; then the Star of David, with the two opposite triangles; the swastika, with its two opposing lines, an ancient Hindu symbol for well-being and prosperity before it was stolen and misused; the moon and the star of Islam; and the yin and yang of Daoism.

Every sign seemed to say that the opposites of good and bad, light and dark did not cancel each other out but coexisted in our Creator. Gems of wisdom from Carl Jung's work came to mind. He had said that the opposites in us come from God,³ and I was now literally seeing the truth of his words. Again, I thought of Mammoth Caves and the crayfish that thrived in the dark. Everything is sacred. Everything has life and the seeds of possibility.

In helping me honor the dark chapters of my own story, the pilgrimage, with its insights, had made me whole again. I looked around. More people were in the church now, scattered across the circle. I got up and tiptoed outside to find Simi.

We would soon be leaving for her home in the kibbutz for the last part of my stay.

* * *

Months later, I received a video from Simi. The church at Tabgha had been renovated and reopened, and she had visited it for me. She walked me through its beautiful length and breadth, ending with the words, "This is until you come here yourself."

My eyes filled up as I watched the video, grateful for my beloved friend's gesture. She had completed my visit to the Holy Land and, at the same time, awakened the perennial pilgrim in me. I knew I would be back.

But for now, my responsibilities needed me at home.

---

3   The actual quote by Carl Jung is, "All opposites are of God, therefore man must bend to this burden; and in so doing he finds that God in his 'oppositeness' has taken possession of him, incarnated himself in him. He becomes a vessel filled with divine conflict."

CHAPTER REFLECTIONS

1. Ani Pema discusses the human tendency to interpret "pain as punishment and pleasure as a reward." Examine your stories of struggle to see your relationship with pleasure and pain. Can you view your pleasant memories as gifts and the unpleasant memories as precious invitations for growth? Try simply sitting with the joy and the pain, without judgment.

2. Make a list of the earthly defeats in your life and recognize the transformation they brought about in you. What blessings came to you from these struggles?

CHAPTER 20

THE VIRTUE OF SELF-CARE

INSIGHT #18
Inner work is also outer work.

I WAS GRADUALLY GETTING MORE and more comfortable with myself. It had been a few months since I had retired my inner critic from the role of mediator between my inner child and inner adult and replaced her with the wise and loving God of the *Gita*. Even so, the tendency to focus on perfection ran deep, and my knee-jerk reactions still mostly came from the old setup. Each time I sensed the harshness in the climate within, I would breathe in divine intervention and let go of my need for self-improvement.

Even with the challenging situations of life, I adopted a new approach. I would begin by journaling my struggles, read them back, and ask myself, *What would Krishna say to this?* Then I would imagine him, the God of my heart, sitting in front of me. His appearance was like the pictures that we worshipped, and he was looking at me kindly, his eyes smiling. Together, we would revisit the storyline, and, as I saw it with a clear head and heart, the answer to my question would emerge. Over time, I got better and better at this and often surprised myself with the insights that came forth.

Yet there were times when there was no answer to that question. Krishna was silent—at least in the moment. Then, in the days that followed, the answer would reveal itself in unexpected places. Often, when teaching a class or during a one-on-one interaction, someone would bring up the very issue I was struggling with that day. In the course of our discussions, the way out would become very clear to me. I would jokingly say it was a "buy one, get one free" scheme in which the student was buying the session and the teacher was getting it for free!

As I kept up with my own inner work while also offering psychospiritual counsel to others, the interconnectedness of our separate worlds was becoming undeniable. In a single week, I would listen to many different, yet similar, stories. Almost identical themes and struggles were unfolding at the same time. It was as though there was a single energy expressing itself in different bodies and lives, like a synchronized ballet with many dancers. Then, one morning, an interesting incident occurred, taking my understanding to a whole new level.

I was getting myself ready to leave for the studio and had just come out of the shower when the sight of my bare body suddenly brought on a tremendous sense of my own mortality. A wave of deep sorrow swept over me with the realization that I would have to leave this body and all those connected with it. Overwhelmed with grief, I broke down and wept. My head watched with disbelief. This had come out of nowhere.

"Hurry up, we have a class to teach," my head went on, but I needed to quell the waves within me first. I hugged myself and waited, breathing mindfully. Eventually, after getting dressed, I set out to begin my day.

Arriving at the studio, I was surprised to see my dear student Erica waiting for me. We didn't have an appointment. After I greeted her and Patti, who was my studio manager, Erica and I headed to the room where I met people for individual counsel. She closed the door behind us, waiting while I put my things away and settled down. Then she blurted, "Ramaa, I just learned I have cancer! I know you have a class to teach, but I needed a safe place to cry."

Now it was she who broke down.

Erica was in her early forties and mother to two young children. As I gathered her in my arms, my eyes filled with tears too. My heart was breaking for her, but my head was noticing a deeper connection. It was not even half an hour earlier that I had felt this same energy of grieving life's impermanence in my own body. Did my emotions attract this, or did this upcoming meeting attract my emotions? Or were we all together in ONE big huddle, bigger than I had realized?

I had come a long way in my journey with my emotions. Raised to believe they were a sign of weakness, I had rejected them at first. Then I had taken responsibility for my feelings, believing them to be my own. I had learned to digest, regulate, and release my fears. Over time, I had learned that my emotions were rooted much deeper in shared experiences with my family and ancestors, whose unfinished business I had inherited. But now I was realizing that my emotions and thoughts came from an even deeper, much larger database.

Although I had read and reflected on the great Thich Nhat Hanh's teachings on interbeing, my own personal experiences were helping me realize the truth of our wider interconnectedness. In the months and weeks that followed my experience with Erica, I began paying close attention to my own feelings as I tried to understand the struggles and fears of those around me.

Our world felt like a forest rooted in the soil of our shared consciousness, with the trees representing each of us. We have our own place on the ground, and our roots are deeply intertwined beneath the surface. We draw from a common repository and contribute to it, which makes each tree as important as the forest itself. The personal contributes to the collective, and vice versa.

In the light of my understanding, I revisited the basic values I was raised with: generosity, kindness, compassion, and so on. I had seen these as values that maintain social order. But now I realized these norms are important because every choice affects our common ground. When someone chooses hatred and violence toward oneself or another, the shared soil is infused with toxins that seep into every tree. Our joys and sorrows impact others, even when they do not know about it. Sooner or later, what's going on with anyone impacts everyone.

The inner work, or the Yoga of self-love, is to cultivate these ethics in our service to the world. Each one is a choice that, like an asana, can be mastered through practice. Taking responsibility for our wounds and applying the teachings to heal, forgive, and open our hearts not only lifts us up but also contributes to making the world a happier place for everyone. Watering a single tree in the forest nurtures the soil everywhere.

In counseling people who were struggling to set right their marriages, their families, or even the world, I began encouraging them to start with their own emotional self-care. Well begun, as the saying goes, is half done already. Putting out the fires of our own fears regarding a situation changes the climate all around and enables us to make good choices.

Going outside without doing the work of healing our inner child is like grocery shopping on an empty stomach. We try to fill up the emptiness within by buying into unnecessary stories and drama. And just like when we shop from a state of fullness, addressing our own pain first allows us to choose wisely for ourselves and, thereby, for everyone.

I came across a quote by the Dalai Lama saying that the Western woman would save the world. The way I understood it, *womanhood* does not refer as much to gender as to one's feminine side. Only those who are in touch with their emotions and enjoy the freedom and privileges of the West could do the inner work to save our planet. Through inner work, we rewrite our past, present, and future, uncovering and releasing memories that don't serve us anymore, challenging limiting thoughts that keep us in repetitive patterns, and reimagining our future to open it up. Like Andy Dufresne, the lead character in *The Shawshank Redemption*, we need to chip away, little by little, at the prisons that lock us in, then make our way to freedom. By releasing ourselves, we raise the consciousness on the planet. Ramana Maharishi, the great Indian sage, said, "Your own self-realization is the greatest service you can render the world."

My insights changed my approach to work as well. Previously, I had believed my mission was to awaken as many people as possible. Now, I realized that making a meaningful difference for even a few individuals is a contribution to everyone. Filled with a new inspiration, I decided it was time for another pilgrimage.

CHAPTER REFLECTIONS

1. When faced with a problem you cannot solve, use your imagination to invite and open up to divine counsel. It could be your personal god/goddess or any symbol of the mystery. Put forth the question on your mind, and see what comes up then and in the days that follow. Keep your mind open to receiving guidance.

2. Make your emotional well-being and self-care a priority in your life. When faced with a problem concerning a friend or a family member, first address your own worst fears regarding the situation. When you release your fears, you are helping them as well.

CHAPTER 21

ANOTHER PILGRIMAGE

INSIGHT #19
When the self is ready, the mirror appears.

MOTHER'S CANCER WAS GETTING worse even though she had been fighting it valiantly since it had returned eight years prior. Having opted out of all traditional treatments, she had instead chosen alternative remedies, much against the family's wishes. Miraculously, she had survived, even outliving our father, who had passed away three years earlier. But she was getting more and more frail, and we had begun to suspect she was entering the last chapter of her battle.

I struggled between wanting to be with her and needing to be in the US for my own family and sangha. I began making frequent short visits, seizing every opportunity to be with her for a few days each time. My classes in the US took on a new schedule to allow for my travels, and students helped by providing meals for my husband and children.

One day after class, Pam, a wonderfully creative member of our community, asked me about my family in India and shared her longings to visit India herself. Like many others in our community, Pam was a certified Yoga teacher and had read extensively about India's spiritual traditions.

"Can you take us with you on one of your trips, Ramaa?" Pam asked. Then she added for more effect, "Traveling to India with you is on my bucket list!"

I smiled and nodded, promising her I would think about it.

Since Mother's illness had gotten worse, I had told her I would reward her with a visit for every birthday she made it to, even as I wondered each time if it would be her last. Mother's next birthday was some seven months away, in February, which is a great month to visit India.

An idea was forming—that of taking my sangha on a pilgrimage to India and combining it with a celebration of Mother's birthday. I ran the plan by Mother and Usha. Both of them thought it would bring cheer to everyone in my family and be a good end to the pilgrimage.

This was not the first time I would be taking a group to India. Ten years earlier, when my sangha was much smaller, I had led another group with help from Shama Kapur, a friend from the Indian community who owned a travel business in Chicago. Thanks to her team, both in the US and India, we had enjoyed a memorable visit. To get started on this new undertaking, I reached out once again to Shamaji, as I liked to call her (the *-ji* is added out of respect for an elder or in more formal situations).

For this second trip, there were eventually thirty-seven of us making the journey. Shamaji handled all the arrangements and even decided to travel with us to make things easier. We met as a group to discuss our travel schedule and the significance of each place we would visit. I worked on preparing the group emotionally and spiritually for the trip, comparing the country of my birth with the country we were living in.

"India is like an old woman, while America is young," I said. "Old women do not have the freshness or the confidence of youth. They sometimes look and smell bad, but when you pause and look into their eyes, you will find the love and wisdom that come only with age. Try and go beyond your five senses where necessary, so you can capture and feel India's soul."

* * *

My sangha and I had been traveling in India for twelve days, and the last part of our trip was coming to an end. The past days had been both exhilarating and difficult. Exhilarating because of the incredible places we had visited, difficult because several members of the trip picked up a virus. Fortunately, it was nothing serious, and people recovered in a short time. Shamaji supported the group with her strong presence and her local connections every place we went.

One of the highlights of our travels so far had been Bodh Gaya, the place where Gautam Buddha attained Nirvana. At the heart of this place stands a large fig tree. Believed to be a direct descendant from the original tree beneath which the Buddha sat, it is known as the Bodhi tree, or the Tree of Awakening.

The morning was bright and sunny as pilgrims from around the world populated the wide expanse surrounding the tree. Despite the bustle, the place felt peaceful. Our group found a quiet spot and settled down to meditate, tuning in to the indelible presence of the great teacher. The eight-fold path of Buddhism reminded me of the eight beatitudes of Jesus, which had touched me the previous year. Once again, I felt the ubiquitous thread between faith traditions.

Before this, we had visited Sarnath, where Buddha's sangha lived hundreds of years ago. The ruins of their living quarters made history tangible. We sat on the well-maintained lawns surrounding the excavations, reflecting on the past and trying to follow in the footsteps of those who had traveled these paths before us.

Our travels also took us to the ancient temples of Khajuraho, whose erotic sculpture sparked much conversation and thought. We marveled at those who had so beautifully integrated sexuality into art, religion, and everyday life. Although I had been raised in India, I had not been raised with the culture of finding beauty in sexuality. And just like me, many others on the trip came from families with similar inhibitions around physical pleasures.

The temple tours included a sound and light show that brought to life the history of a bygone era. We sat together for hours after the show ended, talking about sexuality till late into the night. It was reminiscent of days when we were all high schoolers. Now in midlife, we were conjuring up a new morality that made room for the vagaries of human desire.

And then we went to the city of Varanasi, which is on the banks of the river Ganges. Varanasi is the Jerusalem of Hinduism because of its religious importance. During the course of its habitation of over 3,000 years, the holy town has played host to many great teachers, saints, and seers. Millions have prayed, meditated, and drawn inspiration at this site, where the melting snow from the Himalayas cascades down powerfully as the mighty river Ganges. Mythology describes the river as the forgiving mother, in whose waters of compassion our wounds and mistakes are washed away. Lovingly called Mother Ganga by the locals, the Ganges is the most beloved river in the country.

I had taken a dip in the Ganges a few times in my life, letting go of whatever had been bothering me then. Each time, I had risen from the waters inspired, believing the river was giving me a chance to start over. Bringing the group here for this morning ritual was an important part of the itinerary, and I was grateful for this precious opportunity to share a faith tradition close to my heart.

It was early, with the sun just rising. Most of our group members were there, braving the cold and fear of water pollution only because this meant a great deal to me. The plan was to offer worship to the river before entering the sacred waters.

I began by explaining the close connection Hinduism made between God and nature.

"At its foundation, Hinduism has the ancient Vedas, the revelations that were received, remembered, and passed down for thousands of years. The teachings hold that there are two sides to the truth. Purusha, the masculine principle, and prakriti, the feminine expression of the principle. Purusha, or Spirit, is nothing without its expression in Mother Nature."

They had heard me teach this concept in class before. Now I wanted to show them how it translated into religious practice.

"Rivers in India are seen as feminine energies coming forth from that single source. No two rivers are the same. Each river has its own name, mythology, significance, and character. Some flow gently, some flow forcefully. Some flow through forests with healing herbs and are believed to be therapeutic. Each one has its own journey. Sometimes, a river joins another; sometimes, it separates from one. But no matter what its course, the river is water, and that remains unchanged."

I paused, distracted by the flutter of pigeons close to us as a man was throwing out seeds to feed the birds, a common ritual to please the gods. I smiled, but a pang went through me as I realized how much I had missed the simple sights that were part of life here.

Returning my attention to my group, I continued. "It is the same with our mountains. Each mountain range in India has a local story and is assigned distinct characteristics. The ancient Hindus gave us a wonderful way to understand that although everything in nature is one with a single source, each expression has its unique energy. We can extend this idea to each of us as well. We are all divine, yet differently so. Knowing our unique strengths and peculiarities helps us accept ourselves and show up as we are."

One of the ladies spoke up. It was Jenny, our group's photographer. "Is it true that there are thirty-three million gods and goddesses in Hinduism?"

"Yes, it is, although I do not know them all!"

"Why are there so many?" she wanted to know.

"I like to imagine the reason is because that was the population at the time, and each person was a deity in themselves. But historically, it is because Hinduism is a very old religion," I explained. "It is born out of many groups and tribes that lived in or migrated to the region. While they all embraced monotheism, each group or tribe brought its own gods and practices with them. Over time, different ideologies were debated and then integrated into a single fold. In fact, even the name 'Hinduism' came from the British in later years, referring to the civilization around the river Indus, which is now in neighboring Pakistan."

As we were sitting on an old cement floor, near steps that led to the banks, I noticed a few people around us, immersed in their own worship of Mother Ganga but casting curious glances our way.

To start the morning's worship, I began singing a hymn to the Ganges, handing out copies of the lyrics with translation for others to follow. We prayed together in preparation to descend into the waters.

"Think of what you want to release and leave behind, from this lifetime and also from those we might have lived in the past," I encouraged them.

Then we took the gentle plunge together, our hearts and intentions united as one.

I was feeling very emotional, thinking of so much that I had become ready to set free since the last time I had come to the Ganges. With lessons learned and wounds healed, my huddle was ready, at last, to let go of all the unhappy memories and regrets of the past.

As we emerged from the river, we were cold and pressed close to each other as we walked back, feeling grateful for the time-honored ritual that had given us this renewal of life and an opportunity for a fresh start.

* * *

Later that evening, we assembled in a beautiful room the hotel had provided for our group meetings. The next day, we would leave for our resort in Bengaluru, where Mother and Usha would join us for the last part of our travels. I led the discussions and meditation for the evening, then walked the group through the next day's schedule, as per usual, reminding them to be on time.

"Our flight to Bengaluru is at noon, so we will all need to be ready to leave for the airport at ten o'clock. Pack your suitcases and leave them outside your door at nine thirty. Don't get into trouble with Shamaji!"

Gentle laughter rippled through the group; each of us had become fond of our friendly yet tough travel leader. Having led many such groups before, she always had an eye on the local weather and traffic conditions, and she drew firm lines that we all had to adhere to.

"Ramaa, before you wrap up, we have something we want to share," said Kristen.

Kristen was one of the quieter women in the group, but her warm and sweet nature made her everyone's favorite person. I had known her for at least ten years and treasured our connection.

"What is it, my dear Kris?"

I sensed some excitement in the room as she got up from the back and made her way to me, carrying what looked like a big book.

Handing it to me, Kris said, "Since your mother's birthday is coming up, we all put together a little gift for her. And we'd like to show it to you now."

"That is so very sweet!" I said, feeling touched by the gesture as I reached for the book.

Opening it, I realized it was an album of letters and photos. Some pictures were self-portraits of these women, and others showed their children or families. The letters were addressed to Mother.

When I began reading the first one, Kristen interrupted. "These are letters from each of us to your mother, telling her what you have brought into our lives and thanking her for the gift of your presence. You can keep them with you tonight if you would like to read them first."

As I glanced through them quickly, a lump was forming in my throat.

When I finally managed to find my voice, it was to ask the burning questions on my mind. "Whose idea was this? When did you get this all together? How did you know my mother's first name?"

It had been Kristen's idea, and everyone had jumped right in. Overwhelmed with love and gratitude, I returned the book and asked them to give it to Mother on her birthday, which was a couple of days away. She and I would read the letters together.

Back in my room, I was still in a daze and wondered how Mother would receive their gift. I was struggling to receive it myself, and was barely able to sleep. It was Rumi who said, "Show a mirror to a loved one so she may fall in love with herself." My sangha had shown me a mirror so beautiful that I feared to own it, lest I damage it. In all my years, I had never received such a delightful reflection of myself. Perhaps I had not been ready. I tossed and turned in exhilaration. Digesting one's light is just as challenging as digesting one's darkness.

Somewhere in the early hours of morning, Mother Ganga rescued me. Images of the river dancing along her way appeared behind my tired eyelids. It was as if she was gently whispering into my ears, "Release the shame, release the honor. It is all just water. You cannot add to it. You cannot take away from it."

I heaved a sigh of relief. There was nothing for me to do but go with the flow. The river of time would wash it all away anyway. I finally relaxed into my being, reflecting on how it would be good to reunite with Mother and my family the next day.

Smiling at the thought, I fell asleep.

CHAPTER REFLECTIONS

1. Sacred places are powerful centers of healing. Travel broadens the mind. Taking time off for a pilgrimage supports your journey of transformation. Make time to explore sacred places to see what inspires you. Plan a pilgrimage, even if only for a few days by yourself or with a loved one or your sangha. Set your intentions, carry your journal and prayer accessories, and get going!

2. A pilgrimage doesn't have to take you across the world. It can be some quiet time with nature, a time of prayer and contemplation, even if it is in your favorite local church or temple. Whatever you designate as a pilgrimage can be one. It is the faith and the spirit of the pilgrim that make a difference.

CHAPTER 22

COMING FULL TRIANGLE

INSIGHT #20
*The sangha is the third between our
human self and life's challenges.*

I HAD ONLY A FEW hours of sleep but woke up feeling quite calm and rested, noticing a happy anticipation about introducing my sangha and my family to each other. I was glad to see my emotions around Mother's gift had settled down. I was neither worried about not being worthy of it nor attached to how Mother would view me upon reading it. My only feelings were warmth and gratitude. So far, so good.

* * *

After arriving in Bengaluru that afternoon, we headed to the resort, where we met Usha, who told us Mother was resting. Shamaji had organized a city tour, and many in our group left right away to visit some of the local attractions.

Usha led me to one of the resort's larger cottages, which she and I would be sharing with our mother.

When I saw Mother, my heart sank, as she had become more frail than I could ever have imagined. The cancer had ravaged her body. But, as usual, she was putting on a brave front and wanted to know the details of my recent travels. I followed her cue and shared some entertaining stories.

***

The next day was a gorgeous morning and Mother's birthday, the event the entire visit had been planned around. Mother was eager to meet my co-travelers. She, Usha, and I got ready and headed out to meet the group for breakfast.

The central lounge and dining room were located within easy walking distance from the cottages. It was a well-maintained resort with beautiful lawns and flowering plants. I glanced at Mother as we walked, and I realized I still missed seeing the big red dot, the bindi, on her forehead, which she had replaced with a smaller black one, the sign of widowhood. Tradition forbids widows from applying the red dot, believed to be an auspicious sign of marriage. People do not strictly adhere to those rules today. But, amid protests from Usha and me, Mother had insisted on staying true to the tradition when Dad passed away. It saddened me all over again to see it, yet her sari, her hair, and her style were impeccable, as always. Despite her emaciated body, she carried herself with a presence that could fool anyone into believing she was stronger than she looked.

Over breakfast, each member of my sangha introduced herself to Mother. She had always been a little intrigued about these women from another culture who were so close to her daughter. I sensed its presence today, even as she greeted everyone with warmth and affection.

We all moved into the lounge. Mother sat between Usha and me on a larger couch while the rest of the group sat in chairs, settled on the floor, or stood.

Usha threw Mother a worried look, since each meal usually left her in pain and discomfort. But our mother maintained a stoic front and smiled brightly at the group.

Kristen handed her the gift.

Mother reached for the book, slowly glancing through the initial pages. Then she looked at me as her eyes filled up with tears.

In response to her unspoken question, I shook my head gently and explained. "I had no clue they were doing this. It was a surprise for me as well."

She read a few letters, then looked up at the waiting group of ladies. I could see she was struggling for words. With a voice full of emotion, Mother said, "I really don't know what to say. Thank you very much for this gift. I am so proud of my daughter. Both Ramaa and Usha are teachers, and I always feel very happy to know they are helping others."

I listened quietly, remembering conversations over the years in which she had confessed she didn't quite understand what my work was all about! In her pragmatic way, she had even wondered why people would get together to talk about their feelings when they could be doing more "useful" things with their time. In any case, I could see she was genuinely touched by the love and care that had gone into the gift.

The ladies chatted with her for some more time, asking about her health and her work at the hospital. And then it was time for them to leave. They were off to the nearby city of Mysuru for a day trip, leaving me to spend Mother's birthday with her at the resort. Usha also left to run some errands while Mother and I retired to our room.

We read the letters together. Mother took them in one by one, peering closely at the photographs.

"These letters are extraordinary," she said when the last one was read. "I cannot even imagine the kind of relationships you have built."

"Yes," I agreed. "These are some truly awesome women here. I feel very fortunate."

"They feel that way too. I can tell from their letters that you have touched their lives deeply." She looked up at me. "I am truly proud of you."

I had wanted to hear these words for a very long time. Every ear in my huddle was awake, open, and listening. I remained quiet, capturing this moment to savor later, afraid that saying something might disturb the energy in the room.

"The connection you share with these women feels like a sisterhood from another lifetime," she said.

I spoke then. "It certainly feels that way. We are close-knit and have supported each other through some big challenges. Although coming from entirely different backgrounds and cultures, deep down, we share the same fears, the same wounds, and the same pain. There have been some unbelievable conversations in our sangha."

"Your generation is different from mine," Mother said. "We never talked about our pain, at least not in a group like this. We believed hard work and education would bring success. And success would take care of all the pain."

I was happy to be having this conversation with her. The birthday gift from my sangha had given us this precious opportunity to talk about our emotional lives without the past tensions.

"Well," I said, "success does not make the pain go away. It simply puts a bandage around it. Our group is living proof of that. We are all educated, successful, and reasonably affluent. But we have discovered that nothing and nobody can really make the pain go away. In that sense, I am grateful to you for closing the door on those conversations between us. At the end of the day, each of us has to address our own personal wounds and release them through whatever way works for us. If we don't, we end up passing it down to the next generation."

"Do you think that is what I did? Is your emotional pain my legacy?" Mother asked, her now sharp gaze focused on my face.

Although she had been recognized for her success at work and won several awards, I knew that her role as a mother meant the most to her. She needed my assurance that she had not failed. I struggled, conflicted by my desire to set her mind at rest at this late stage of her life, yet wanting her to know that she had not always met my emotional needs.

As I paused and breathed, it was suddenly clear to me that she had done the best she knew how. Whatever pain her choices had caused me were because of messages she herself had internalized. She also had been wounded along the way, but had never taken the time to heal. I replied slowly, choosing my words thoughtfully.

"I don't know whether you gave me my emotional pain or if I was born with it, Mother. Perhaps you also inherited it, but hid it under your many accomplishments. In any case, my emotional baggage is the best gift you could have given me for the growth, the friendships, and the depth it has brought to my life."

"Looks like I did something right after all."

The lingering pain of parental guilt in her words touched me deeply. Having had plenty of that with respect to my own children, I felt compassion for Mother and for all mothers who struggle with the gap between who they are and who they think they should be for their children. It is a discussion we have had many times in our sangha.

"Oh, Mother, you did a lot more right than wrong, believe me! You taught me to work hard, play fair, and take responsibility. That was what your generation was meant to give us, and you did. These women were raised on the other side of the world, but they received the same messages. I realize now that it was just the consciousness of your times. The work of adding emotional intelligence to the human journey fell to our generation. Our wounds were our wake-up calls to the work we were meant to do. God knows our children will have their own wounds, revealing to us what needs to unfold in the future."

I succeeded in settling her down with this effort. She looked tired and not interested in going any further.

"Well, you have surely given me a great gift this birthday, and I am glad you have found the friends who understand and support you. I am going to rest now."

Putting the album aside, she settled down for a nap just as Usha returned from her errands. The two of us quietly stepped out for a walk in the cool, crisp air. With Mother out of earshot, we talked about her health and the challenges Usha was facing in supporting her.

I empathized with my sister. Elder care is not easy, and she had done a lot of that in her life. First with her husband's parents and then with ours. Usha was also a Yoga teacher and had her own sangha. I asked her how her work was going.

"Not great," she replied. "I have reduced it to a bare minimum. Between running the household and taking care of Mother, there is not much time to spare for deep contemplation."

I said nothing, feeling a pang of guilt for living on the other side of the world without these challenges. After a moment, she added, "I can see your work is thriving though."

"Yes, it is. I am both teacher and student with these women, and I feel like together, we have healed wounds from many lifetimes."

"I understand. Good for you," said Usha. I stole a quick glance at her, wondering if I was missing a tinge of sarcasm. But there was none. She added simply, "I sense I have to do that same work myself. Unlike you, I do not have the luxury of time and distance now. I will get to it someday, no doubt. My duty right now is to take care of our mother. Other things will simply have to wait."

For years, there had been an undercurrent of tension between us over the responsibilities that had ended up in Usha's lap when I moved to America. Since our brother also lived in a different city, she was the only one who had been available to take care of our parents and their needs.

Her words, carrying no regret or blame, helped me listen with openness and respect. Her emphasis on duty and her ability to compartmentalize her emotions to focus on that duty reminded me that we had been raised by the same mother. I also saw that my own work had been possible because Usha had taken care of things in India.

As we walked back to our room, I sincerely hoped that my work had eased the pain in our family pool at a deeper level. I prayed it had made Usha's life easier, even if in ways she may never realize.

***

We spent one more day at the resort, and my brother-in-law, Usha's husband, joined us, along with my niece and Usha's new granddaughter. So did my brother and his partner. The whole family was there now. The ladies from my sangha were busy receiving traditional massages and other herbal treatments on this final day while I was holding on to every minute with Mother.

At the end of every trip to India, I would leave with mixed feelings—sad to leave my family and country of birth but eager to return to my family in Chicago and my regular routine. On this visit, though, there was more.

I knew in my bones that Mother would not have another birthday, and my heart was hurting with the thought. My life and, indeed, India itself would not be the same without her. Time was ending a chapter of my life, and there was no stopping it.

The trip was over. It was time to say our goodbyes and board the bus to the airport. The luggage was loaded, and one by one, the women in our group bid Mother and the rest of my family farewell before boarding the bus. I embraced Mother one more time before joining them.

As the bus started to move, we looked out our windows at my family waving us off.

Mother's birthday had been a great celebration. I continued to look out the window until the figures of my family faded out of sight, then I turned to those around me.

Kristen was sitting by my side. "Are you okay?" she asked gently.

"Yes, thank you." I nodded and smiled. The sound of excited chatter surrounded us. It had been a great vacation, but everyone was ready to go home. And so was I.

As I looked fondly at their happy faces, Mother's words returned to my mind. "A sisterhood from another lifetime," she had said. Indeed. Over the years, we had cultivated a genuine connection, deepening it from simple friendship to a more conscious solidarity. Love had helped us heal and make peace with what could not be changed. We had propped one another up and found our unique gifts. Committing ourselves to retiring generational patterns, we were moving forward with a new vision, applying and often reinterpreting the teachings from various faith traditions.

I had come up with the name "Full Bloomed Lotus" for my work when I had moved my self-awareness groups out of my home and into a rented studio in the neighborhood. It was not a traditional Yoga studio. I had wanted to create a sangha for self-awareness and had been looking for a word that would describe my vision. After pondering the question for several days, I was meditating one morning when I saw the image of a lotus pushing through the muddy waters, unfolding its petals. Although I did not know it as clearly then, over the years, I had come to see the divine feminine at the center and all of us as petals of the lotus. Drawn together by a shared yearning and rising through the messy situations in our individual lives, we had each been lifted by the center to open up and shine.

Now, all at once, it occurred to me that in the struggle between Mother's pragmatic outlook and my soulful one, our sangha had been the third. It had allowed the space for both Mother and me to be our authentic selves, with our energies flowing in the direction they needed to. Thanks to the surprise birthday gift, Mother had finally seen and appreciated the importance of my work and the role of my emotionality. Our conversation had cleared the air and restored our connection.

My heart swelled with joy and gratitude.

Mother and I had completed our souls' work together. We had come full triangle.

The Sangha at the Taj Mahal, Agra, India

Worshipping the Ganges at dawn

Mother, so brave and strong despite her emaciated frame

With Mother and Usha on the right (taken on an earlier visit)

EPILOGUE

AFTER TEN MONTHS AND two more visits, Mother breathed her last breath. My last time with her was less than a month before she passed. In our time together, she assured me I had done my duty as a daughter very well. As for herself, in her classic style, Mother made all the arrangements she could for her own passing, down to the smallest detail. In the weeks and months that followed, we met dozens of people who told us how much she had helped them with her connections and generosity.

Although it has been over seven years since she passed, I have not gone a day without thinking about Mother. I can no longer pick up the phone and speak with her as I used to, but her voice, her words, and her energy are with me all the time—sometimes supportive, often critical, but always there and available, just as she was in her lifetime.

The last several years of Mother's life were a struggle for both of us. She had fought her cancer; I had battled my demons. Her victory was through release from her diseased body; mine was through release from old, limiting beliefs. Both our journeys moved us forward, although in different directions.

I had come to understand that we can't go far in any of our pursuits without first addressing the wounds and needs of the younger self. In my new spirituality, I see the inner child as our light—our very soul—and believe that our daily sadhana lies in nurturing, protecting, and shining this light in our unique ways. My mission became sharing the inner work of integrating the conflicting voices within—all under the watchful and supportive presence of a loving God.

I invested Mother's gifts of self-discipline and hard work into my vision, creating programs for staying connected to and working with one's emotions. In the years that followed, I founded a nonprofit to share these teachings and techniques with a wider audience, particularly children, even as I continued to deepen my relationship with the little girl in red. Many from my sangha were now leaders in their own right, and I supported them in moving forward with their individual missions.

Together, we were and are doing our bit to make this world a better place.

And somewhere in the world beyond, I know Mother is watching and cheering us on.

BONUSES

#1

The ABCDE's of The Yoga of Self-Love: Ramaa lays out foundational daily practices to stay connected to and work with your inner child.

#2

Join Ramaa in a "huddle meditation" to unite the various selves within and strengthen your inner "Team Spirit."

Download your bonuses here:

ACKNOWLEDGMENTS

WHOEVER SAID, "MANY HANDS make light work," knew what they were talking about. It has indeed taken many hands and hearts working together to bring into form the wisdom and insights contained in this book, and I would like to acknowledge them all. Starting at the very beginning, I thank my dear friend Helen Sweitzer for believing in me and my gifts even when I didn't know I had any and for encouraging me twenty-five years ago to start what eventually became Full Bloomed Lotus Center for Self-Awareness.

My sincere thanks to all the "petals" of Full Bloomed Lotus for bringing their light, trusting me with their stories, and exploring with me the joys and challenges of being human. You have all helped me understand what it takes to truly heal and come into full bloom.

Although I had been teaching for many years, I needed a whole new legion of angels when I finally decided to write this book. I am very grateful for each of them. Marie Curran of WriteByNight was my first guide, encouraging me to write in my own authentic voice even as I tried (and failed) to mimic other writers whose styles I admired and envied! Rebecca Maizel of Yellow Bird Editors was brilliant in directing my writing toward a larger audience and helping establish a sequence in the narrative that flowed better than when we started. Nicole Sholly of Pithy WordSmithery worked patiently with me as together we cut my original work down to a more digestible size. A big thank-you to Howard VanEs of Let's Write Books, Inc. for helping me with the publishing part of the journey and holding a steady vision for the book while I experienced the final birthing pangs.

I cannot thank enough the many, many women in our community who have encouraged and helped me with this, my maiden venture as a writer: first, my dear friend and sister on the journey, Sharon Bussell, for sharing her knowledge and wisdom as a psychotherapist, for our endless conversations contrasting the Eastern and the Western approaches to mental/emotional health, for listening to my every story and insight as it unfolded, and then later patiently reading each chapter of this book as I wrote it. I also owe a debt of gratitude to my beta readers, who read the book in its original and unedited version and gave me their thoughtful feedback; to my close-knit Saturn Sisters group for their steady friendship; and to so many others who have been following the progress of this book and assuring me of their support.

And last but certainly not least, I would like to express my heartfelt gratitude to my family. The midlife story really begins at home, and I am deeply grateful to my dear husband, Krish, and our children, Anish and Amrita, for signing up at a soul-ular level to be here for me, to bear witness to my journey—all parts of it, the good, the bad, and the ugly—and for loving me through it all.

ABOUT THE AUTHOR

RAMAA KRISHNAN IS THE founder of the Full Bloomed Lotus Center for Self-Awareness. Born and raised in India, she developed a deep spiritual perspective on life and her role in the world. Initially focused on studying and sharing meditation and mindfulness teachings, Ramaa encountered a challenging chapter in her life that led her to question her beliefs and to dig deeper to understand what it truly means to live a life of faith beyond traditional practices.

Ramaa now shares these profound insights through her classes and one-on-one sessions, both in-person and online. She lives in Wilmette, Illinois, with her loving husband and two adult children.

To learn more about Ramaa's ongoing offerings or to join her sangha, visit www. fullbloomedlotus.com or email her at info@fullbloomedlotus.com.

www.ingramcontent.com/pod-product-compliance
Lightning Source LLC
Chambersburg PA
CBHW050748100426
42744CB00012BA/1930